The Tickle Papers

Previous Books by Phyllis Tickle

The Tickle Papers

Parables and Pandemonium

Phyllis Tickle

Abingdon Press / Nashville

THE TICKLE PAPERS

Copyright © 1989 by Phyllis Tickle

This book is printed on acid-free paper.

BOOK JACKET AND BOOK DESIGN BY JOHN R. ROBINSON

Library of Congress Cataloging-in-Publication Data

TICKLE, PHYLLIS.
  The Tickle papers / Phyllis Tickle.
    p.   cm.
  ISBN 0-687-41910-7
  1. Vocation. 2. Grace (Theology) 3. Tickle, Phyllis. I. Title.
  BV4740.T53   1989   88-22650
 248.4—dc19   CIP

MANUFACTURED BY THE PARTHENON PRESS AT
NASHVILLE, TENNESSEE, UNITED STATES OF AMERICA

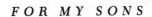

FOR MY SONS

——C O N T E N T S——

T H E   F A M I L Y
T I C K L E

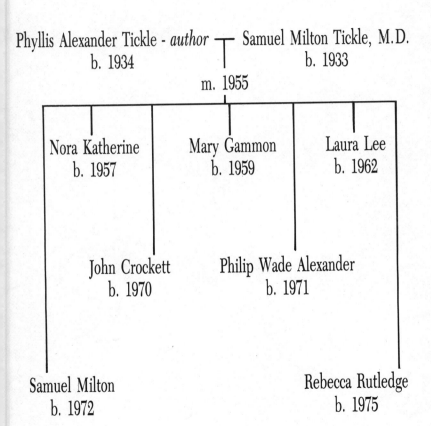

Phyllis Alexander Tickle - *author*   Samuel Milton Tickle, M.D.
b. 1934   b. 1933

m. 1955

Nora Katherine   Mary Gammon   Laura Lee
b. 1957   b. 1959   b. 1962

John Crockett   Philip Wade Alexander
b. 1970   b. 1971

Samuel Milton   Rebecca Rutledge
b. 1972   b. 1975

——FOREWORD——

A book is like a game, a way of crawling out of life in order to look at it without risk. Readers and their authors, even though we all move in the same space, rarely meet. Certainly we never meet inside the dimensions of the book. An author only draws the playing court and sets out the equipment. Then, by the rules of a bigger game, he has to leave the field. After that, there are as many books as there are players, each book different, each book private.

What follows here is a collection of stories, autobiographical and therefore only partially fictive, but still stories. They are the result of my absorption with one term—"vocation." The Tickles caught here are the Tickles I believe I see around my dinner table every night, but the vocation is more subtle . . . a matter of the memory as much as of the eye . . . but a ball well worth chasing.

And one last thing . . . I hope you enjoy the game as much as I have.

CALLED
TO THIS LIFE

1

Called
to This Life

Women keep emotional time, all our life events being posted around anniversaries of the heart rather than of the mind. That's how I know it was 1973; it was Laura Lee's twelfth year and her last in elementary school.

The morning we sent her off for the first full day of that benchmark year was vintage September. The whole world, as far as the eye could see or the imagination could project, was full of useless heat. Even the plants it was supposed to nurture were now seared brown and tired from the abundance of its affections. The sky was that cloudless and raucous blue which is always born of too many days without rain. Only the faintest movement of air teased the trees, and even that was no more than the transient cool of early morning rising to meet the hot, dry air above them.

A good morning to send youngsters off—or as many of them as I legally could—to other occupations. A good day to declare summer over and domestic peace reborn. It was, I thought, going to be a benchmark day.

Accordingly, I waved good-bye with more than my customary enthusiasm as Sam pulled out of the driveway with Laura in tow. A ride to school with Daddy is one of those special indulgences that occur only when one can show demonstrable and compelling reasons for delaying hospital

17

rounds and the beginning of Daddy's patient day. It works, in other words, only when there is snow, sleet, ice, a birthday, a broken appendage, civil disorder, or a brown-eyed little girl who says "Please, Daddy." It was the last one that got him this morning—that and the fact that her arms really were full to the point of ridiculous overload with all the supplies and books we had had to acquire for her since registration the previous Friday. Nobody in his right mind would ever assume that any youngster could make meaningful use of so much stuff, I thought as she went forth into the heat toward the car, books, notebooks, folders, rulers, compasses, pencils, and glue bottles sticking out of every pocket and seam of her.

The older children had already gone off on their respective buses, their schools being way out of walking distance. Rebecca had not yet joined us; she was still over a year away, more a longing than a person at that point. So I was down to just John and Sam junior. Having seen my last two travelers off, I came back into the kitchen and considered my options. What I considered was that I needed a day off, a way to celebrate that glorious event known among mothers as THE FIRST DAY OF SCHOOL.

John was going on four and alarmingly precocious. Unlike his siblings, who had, with the exception of oldest sister Nora, shown a marked aversion to the printed word, he had an avaricious concern with it. He had been twenty-two months old the day he brought me my *Book of Common Prayer* and demanded that I watch while he pointed out and read aloud all the *the's* in the Psalter (I had previously had no idea how many *the's* there are in the Psalter!). I had found the whole experience and those which followed—all the *call's* in the Yellow Pages, for instance—so disconcerting and time-consuming that I damned "Sesame Street" for two weeks before I decided to help myself by finding a preschool program for obnoxious kids. He, therefore, had been in an afternoon "thing," as his father called it, three days a week for almost a year now.

What would happen, I wondered maliciously to myself, if I took Sam junior to the Mother's Day Out at our parish house at the same time that I took John to his "thing" down the street

18

from the church? Lovely, was my answer to myself. Laura would get home first because she would have to walk and that was quicker than the buses, but I could wait until the older children got home and then go pick up the two boys. All things being equal, I should have a blatantly indulgent window of almost three hours alone at home. I would do it.

Eleven-thirty rolled around with all the morning chores cleaned up and both boys fed and watered for their afternoon of social and educational opportunities. I loaded up and delivered each and came back to a serene house in which I promptly fell asleep over a book I had told Sam repeatedly I was dying to read. I was roused by the angry snarl of the doorbell.

I came up from my chair, caught the clock out of the corner of my eye, and put on my mother face. It was 3:20! "Hello, dear. Forget your key?" (I am all maternal innocence faking alertness. Years of experience have taught me that it is best never to let one's guard down; children simply can never be led to understand why parents need sleep too.)

"Yeah. Where were you?" (She is suspicious, I can tell.) "I rang and rang."

"I was upstairs." I let it stop there. It had been on the tip of my tongue to add "working," but even I couldn't go that far.

Oddly enough, she didn't ask, just went straight to the kitchen and threw down her much more reasonable stack of three books, a notebook, and her purse. She went to the refrigerator and got a glass of ginger ale, still without saying anything. I trailed in behind her and made motions toward a salad for supper, thinking she would talk if I did. She didn't. She drank her ginger ale and plowed through the fruit bowl for an apple.

"Did everything go all right today?"

"Yes'm."

"Did you have everything you needed off your list?"

"Sure. We already got it all this weekend. Remember?"

"Well, yes. I just thought we might have missed something."

"Nope. It was all there."

Silence. Here we were, just the two of us, and this child

19

who more than any of them seemed to covet my undiverted attention was totally without words.

"OK," I said as the last of the apple was about to go, "what's wrong?"

"Nothing's wrong," she answered in that angelic softness that was and is her more customary speech form. The sullenness of her entry was gone now, like the heat and thirst that had accompanied it. She was only twelve again and gentle; not yet world tough; not yet ready to handle it all, but still old enough to want the privacy of thinking it over first. Then the tear showed, just one in the corner of one eye, and ran under her glasses so that she had to admit to it in order to wipe it away. That did it. I stopped pretending with the salad and sat down at the table with her.

"All right, now," I said, trying to keep my usually fulsome voice down to the quietness that so becomes hers. "Can you tell me what has gone wrong?"

"Nothing exactly went 'wrong'." She was hesitant, but I could tell it was going to come, given enough help.

"But?" I said.

"Oh, Mama," she wailed. "Do you know what it's like being asked every single year in front of the whole class how many brothers and sisters you have this year?"

"That's it?" I was stunned. "That's the problem?"

"Well, of course it's the problem. Everybody just roars. They all think it's a blast! I get asked every single year, and nobody else ever does. They all have the same number every year. It's just me the teachers ever have to ask, and they ask in every single class. The first question is, 'Did everyone have a good summer?' Then, 'Laura Lee, are there any new brothers or sisters at your house this year?' Or, 'Well, Laura, how's your mother?' Mrs. Tutwiler in math was the worst. She just outright asked me when I was going to have another baby sister. Every class, Mama! *Every* class! And we're not even Roman Catholic, for goodness' sakes!"

Still a bit nonplussed that our emotional emergency was so benign, I struggled for the way in to her distress. "But, Honey, the teachers are all just being friendly. None of them could know that the others had already asked, and besides, they probably really just want to know because they have all taught Nora and Mary and Philip, and they love you and look forward to having the rest of us. It's all right."

"I know." She sighed mightily. "It's just that everyone else laughs at me . . . all the other kids."

"Why?"

"You know why."

I honestly didn't, so I tried again. "No, I don't. Why?"

"Because of where they come from." Her voice was very low, the words tucked into her blouse so that I could barely hear them.

I laughed. I couldn't help myself. As God is my witness, this is the one child whom I would never hurt ever, with whom I almost kill myself at times to be exquisitely cautious, but I couldn't help it. I laughed.

Slowly, as I struggled for my control, she began to lose hers. Through my own relieved merriment, I saw her look up and then grin and then outright smile the first smile of her homecoming. Finally she chuckled. "Well, it's true," she said through her soft laughter. "If you just wouldn't chase Daddy all over the place all the time, it wouldn't happen." That one stopped me dead.

"I do *not* chase your father!"

"Of course you do, when he's not chasing you. It's disgusting!"

I sobered completely and looked her directly in the eye. "Is it really, Laura? Is that what you really think?"

She was startled, I think—one of the few times in our life together, in fact, when I think I ever really startled one of our children. She looked almost as if I had physically struck her for just a moment. Then she shook her head as if in a kind of interior amazement.

"No, m'am," she said eventually. "No m'am, I guess that's not what I think at all. I guess I really think that it's kind of neat." She got up, gathered her books into a stack and, swooping them into her arms, turned to leave the kitchen. Over her shoulder she threw at me, "But it sure makes a heck of a lot of babies."

I caught just the wisp of an impish smile on her face as she

21

and her forbidden impudence beat a hasty retreat up the stairs to her room. So, I thought to myself, the death of another innocence has begun, and went back to the salad, which at this point in the afternoon really was more a necessity than an exercise.

The older kids hit the respective doors about then from their respective buses, and all of Laura Lee's hell broke loose right on schedule. Dutifully and without any real reluctance, I got into the car and fetched home two more merriment-makers to add to the carnival. These two, fortunately, were too tired to be much problem except that John had learned "Exit" that afternoon and cried because we didn't have any at home to show Nora that he really could read it. Otherwise the day wound down very pleasantly after that, its pleasantness in no small part due probably to my nap and everyone else's homework.

That night, sitting in my chair in the bedroom and really reading the book this time in seriousness, I heard Sam coming in from a late call and went down to say a simple "Hello" and "Welcome home." He was half in the refrigerator and half out when I got there, and I patted the half that was out affectionately. The half that had been in came out and returned the affection. From the doorway, a voice said, "See, you're doing it again."

"What does she mean by that?" her father said as he went back into the refrigerator, his words muffled in the leftovers he was considering.

"She means," I said, looking at her standing there in the doorway, "she means that she thinks I should quit chasing you."

"Wrong," he said emphatically as he came out with a cold hamburger patty. He looked her straight in the eye. "Your mother was called to this life."

I don't remember much after that. I know he made his sandwich with that hamburger and I can guess that she probably ate something with him, but I just don't remember the process. I remember only his words, "Your mother was called to this life." As surely as any priest is ordained or any pastor invested, I was likewise—not by those words, but by their terrible accuracy. Sam has always perceived our truths long before I have, but never more succinctly than on that fateful night. A head full of books and words, a heart full of Episcopalian fervor, and a body full of appetites and babies.

What I remember most about that night is the relief of accepting for the first time in my life the fact that they weren't even contradictory elements; that they all could make a perfectly credible whole; and that the resulting whole is a lay Christian. I was at least one possible variation on that ancient theme, "the order of the laity."

It was a discovery that has informed all my life since that night in the kitchen when Laura was twelve and I was invested, typically enough, over a hamburger and a two-day-old bun by the man I had every intention of going to bed with as soon as he was finished eating.

2

Naked
in the Fields

ven if my perception of the lay life as a vocation did not come until fairly late in my own experience, certainly my perception of life as a feast of worldly delights did.

When I was five and almost six, my parents bought a house. It was our first house. It was also to be their only house, but none of us could have known that then.

My father was a college professor, and like many another college professor in the thirties, he was expected to do an untold number of things besides lecturing. One of them was being, with my mother, houseparent to the largest men's dormitory on campus.

There was an apartment on the first floor of the dorm right beyond the front door. The door itself, massive, paned with many lights, and doubled, opened onto a center hall, which ran the length of the whole building, straight back to an identical door well over a hundred feet to the rear.

Twenty-some feet back from the front door there was a kind of false arch or suggestion of an interruption that marked off the houseparents' space from the boys' space. I was never allowed beyond that open and essentially imaginary barrier, nor were the young men allowed to come back once they had passed through it. One of the great mysteries of my early childhood, in fact, was why the same undergraduate who had just walked through the front door and down the hall to his room or to the stairway could not, twenty minutes later, turn around and come back the same way in order to leave. Not so.

Once in the building, a boy must exit by the far door. Should one of the resident scholars need something from the housemaster or the hostess (the titles were as numerous as they were euphemistic), he must ring the bell, which hung on the dorm side of the arch, and be formally admitted before he crossed back into the apartment side of the hallway.

The other truth about the hallway was that it ran not only through the center of the dormitory, but also right through the center of our apartment. Mama's kitchen and dining room were on the left side of the front door. Our living and sleeping quarters were on the right. The reason for this apparent inconvenience was even more burdensome. Mother was expected to oversee and serve certain elegant teas, large receptions, and formal dinners out of the food areas of our home. Keeping our living quarters separate was supposed to give us at least some modicum of a private life.

As a child, of course, I did not perceive, much less appreciate, what a difficulty this must have been for her as a young housewife and mother. What I did perceive was that a boys' dormitory, while it may be unusual, is certainly not an unpleasant place for a girl-child to grow up.

I was the recipient of every kind of indulgence the late adolescent male can contrive to build, make, or invent. Part of the activity was, I am sure, motivated by a desire to get on the good side of the housemaster by favoring his only child. Part of it was loneliness, I imagine, for in the late thirties there was little money even among the affluent for going to and from home, much less for buying young men automobiles to run around in. And part of it was that I was a con artist.

If those years taught me anything at all, they taught me by trial and error and very meaningful reinforcement how to smile sweetly and ask indirectly, but clearly. They also taught me to be very comfortable in the company of males.

As a result of all this, I had the best rubber-tire swing I have ever seen anywhere and I had a complete set of lackeys ready to push it for me at all times. I had the highest and most precarious tree house in Upper East Tennessee. It was hauled, perched, and nailed by four chemistry majors who almost failed their labs trying to finish it for my fourth birthday. I had a mini-swimming pool created by three freshmen who dammed up a campus stream for my sole convenience. I was the only one in the place small enough to fit into it.

I had a lean-to shop of sorts, fashioned outdoors along the bedroom side of our apartment, in which I was allowed to destroy all the worn-out clocks, defunct radios, and burned-up lamps my constituency collected for me. This was not idle destruction, however. It was guided, always by the giver, into elaborate and apparently accurate analyses of how the thing had worked originally and of how it had died—occasionally even of how it was to be fixed. The knowledge of clock works which I thus gained has been of no great value since those days in the dormitory's side yard and the whole structure of radios has changed since solid-state came in, but the rest of the experience has proved invaluable.

Mine, then, was a paradise and I a princess in it until my father lowered the boom when I turned five. When I turned five, the paternal edict came down that I had to give up my almost adult playmates. In the future the young men—as my father called them and as he addressed them in his open letter posted on each floor of Ritter Hall—in the future the young men were to confine their visitations with the housemaster and his family to formal ones in the center hall. Other conversation and contact between the master's family and the dormitory residents were forbidden. Violation of this policy would, regrettably, result in the offender's expulsion from quarters.

At the same time as, and somewhat as a result of, this edict, I was forbidden the use of the center hall unless fully clothed, which, by my father's definition, meant in dress, petticoat, shoes, and socks. In practical application what it meant was that I could not go back and forth to the kitchen with my former ease—no breakfast in my pajamas, no running to find Mama in my panties, no after-dinner snack unless still in my clothes. As a life-style change, it was the pits. There was definitely trouble in paradise.

It never occurred to me, of course, that these restrictions were in my best interests or at least in the best interest of propriety. Nor did it occur to me that they were the very same restrictions and inconveniences that had plagued my parents for several years already. Instead, I remember being distinctly petulant about the whole thing . . . and genuinely miserable about so abrupt a change. In fact, I have never trusted birthdays since.

Whether my mourning posture or my mother's growing weariness was the straw that broke the camel's back, I never knew. Maybe the two combined did the trick. Whatever the reason, my father, just before my sixth birthday, took the bull by the horns and announced to the president that he was taking his family off campus to live. No longer junior faculty (in fact, just recently tenured, that being a third reason for his rebellion, I suspect), he could afford the luxury of personal quarters and the relief of time away from students. We moved.

We moved to the most gigantic house three people were ever asked to occupy. We never did fill it up in all the years that I, and then they alone, lived there. Even after I had grown up and gone, I used to come back to that house and wonder why in the world anybody would want to fool with keeping up that much house. But my mother never wearied of it, and I think she went to her grave still shaped by all those years of keeping house on two sides of a public hall.

Anyway, suddenly we had an enormous and secluded front porch, an entrance hall of sizable proportions for keeping at bay callers whom we did not want to accept into our inner sanctum, a living room the size our dormitory apartment had been, a dining room, a breakfast room, a kitchen, four bedrooms, two baths, a basement, and a massive playroom—this last simply because no one of us could figure out what else to do with the thing. We had run out of room names and needs.

How we filled up such space is a little unclear in my head. I assume, looking back, that we didn't at first, and that my grandparents helped. All I remember is the openness of the place and its vastness.

Day after day, before we moved, my mother and I would go to the new house and direct while workmen steamed off old wallpaper and hung new, sanded floors and re-stained them, pulled up linoleum and laid tile, pried up windows and replaced broken glass. Night after night the three of us would go back after supper for my parents to scrub and clean and paint that which could not be trusted to the workmen.

Eventually we moved into what I recall was still a fairly empty house, its many rooms having consumed our limited furnishings with nairy a burp nor a belch.

It was paradise regained. No one looking. No one between me and the kitchen. No objects between me and running.

When my father shut and bolted the front door behind the last load of movers, I suddenly grabbed my skirt tails, yanked the hateful things over my head, petticoat and all, scuffed off my socks and sandals, dropped my panties, and went racing. To this day, fifty years later, I can recall exquisitely and joyfully the rush of that freedom.

I raced round and round the core of the house, passing through room after room on my way back to start again. Up and down the stairs, round and round the stairwell until, exhausted, I dropped halfway up and laughed and laughed and laughed. I can't remember anything after that. Knowing more about children now, I would suspect that I fell asleep on the riser and got carried off later to my bed. But I do remember in my racing passing my mother and hearing her say to my father, "Let her alone. She's not hurting anything."

I could probably list on my ten fingers the entire catalog of those events, occurring in childhood but surviving into adulthood, which have turned out to be more vivid and more formative in memory than they were in their original life as events. Of those, I could probably list on one hand the few such events which have become icons in my private world as an adult. The day of the racing is one of these latter.

As with all icons, I handle it little but consciously meditate upon it from time to time, as I have here, and believe myself to have been formed by it in some very prognostic and almost architectural way.

In the late seventies, Sam and I moved from the city, where we had had to live while he was building his practice as a pulmonary specialist, to the country where we belonged. Sam continued to drive in and out to the city to practice, but as a family we dropped, with the exception of Daddy's daylight activities, into the patterns and necessities of farm life. We put in a herd and fed ourselves from the garden. We butchered our own beef and canned our own vegetables. I made our bread. We lived, as thousands of generations have lived, from our land.

There are many reasons why folks move from the city to the country. Our move was motivated, at least a little bit, by every one of them. Although the back-to-basics movement of the late sixties was well over by the time we were free to move, we certainly shared its central concern about consumerism and what happens to children who are reared in the fever of that social disease.

Sam had grown up gardening and canning, feeding, and butchering, so our move was a return to earlier and easier ways for him. In addition, we wanted the children—this sounds as if we had been scarred by George Orwell, but so be it—we wanted the children to know those skills it takes to survive on the land should they ever need to. All these things, and many more, were part of our thinking when we began deliberately to look for the life that we found when we bought the Lucy Goose Farm and moved here.

When, however, all of that is said, and it is all true, there still remains the other motivation. One moves to the country to escape. The question, of course, is what.

The inside of a city is, perhaps mercifully, one of the most alone places, the most anonymous places, man can inhabit. Given that, it's a little illogical to say, as many do, that folks move to the country to get away from people. One must be more specific, I suspect, and say that folks move to the country to escape human activity and human conventions, not human intimacies. Like Jonathan Swift, most of us like Tom, Dick, and Harry; it's just humanity we can't abide.

29

Certainly we were no different in this than in any of the other motivators. The greater the density of human population, the greater the level of human activity and the greater the number of rules, covenants, and agreements it takes to govern that activity. With all those children inside, we certainly didn't need congestion outside, and we went to the country, to the out-in-the-middle-of-nowhere, totally-removed-from-humanity country.

For my own part, though, I was still restive. Some part of our move was not yet quite done, some elusive part that would, when I found it, mean the move was complete for me. We had been on the Lucy Goose for a year, more or less, when that time came.

It was a Friday evening, and by some set of circumstances I can no longer reconstruct, Sam and I were alone in the house. I can guess that camp, a spend-the-night, a movie date, a weekend with an older sister, or any number of such possibilities had stripped us of children, at least briefly.

The dishes, such as they were, were done and Sam was reading. Outside the dark had already moved in from the east and was closing down over the last traces of the sun above the river. It was not yet hot, I remember that, and not yet mosquito season. The moon, through the sitting room window, was just beginning to rise. I got up, went to the back door, took off all my clothes, folded them neatly in a stack beside the door, and walked out into the moonlight.

The sun had set entirely, the last vestiges of its light gone now from the western sky. The moon came up quickly above the orchard trees and dappled my skin with its shadows. I looked, even to myself, no different from, indistinguishable from, in fact, the other objects on the patio. I walked out into the yard and then on to the pasture fence, drawn on, with each change of place, by how hidden I was in the light's camouflage.

Sam called and I did not answer, waiting to see if he could discern me, hiding as Eve must have hidden, playing hide-and-seek with her lover. He gave up and went back in, but he must have seen my clothes as he did so, for he came

30

back out immediately, calling as he came. He found me there, still dappled and hiding in the light.

"What in the world are you doing?"

"I'm seeing what it feels like to be naked in the public view of nobody." I was faintly surprised to hear that that was what I was doing, because I really hadn't given the matter any thought up till then, and I was plainly clothed as completely in the moonlight as I will ever be in any cloth garment.

"Well, I don't suppose you're hurting anything," Sam laughed, and suddenly I laughed. Bingo! My mother was standing again in the hallway of the old house, watching me run and saying to my father, "Let her alone. She's not hurting anything." Only this time it was my husband speaking her words. Not hurting anything. Not hurting anything. Not hurting anything. The sweetest freedom of all. Not hurting anything . . . being and being and being, invisible in the light, but not hurting anything with the being. I laughed.

I remembered vaguely how good the laughter had been before, how full and nourishing like potatoes or bread, and it was the same laughter this time as I broke out running, beating him back to the house because I had taken him by surprise and run without announcement.

Still laughing, I got back into my clothes and made us coffee before the first of the children drifted back home, unaware, in their dreaminess, that I had just discovered the meaning of kingdom. I had had to leave it out there where it still waits for me, but I had at least discovered its definition . . . which is just pagan enough so that I suspect no priest will ever be willing to tell them about it, but their middle-aged mama surely can, as I imagine you have already guessed by now.

——— 3 ———

Hen House Truths

Kingdom has many names, of course, not all of them mine and certainly not all of them rural. But a farm is both rural and domestic just as most of Christianity's sources, metaphors, and scriptures are. Because of this, farm life can become an easy and accessible way to expose the truths of the faith to one's children without having to beat them over their reluctant heads with a lot of precepts. At least it seems to have worked that way for us.

John was within a month of being seven when we finally moved to the farm. It was June before his July birthday and still tolerably pleasant outside. Even if it hadn't been tolerably pleasant, he would have been out there anyway, so great was his delight in all the space and life around him.

No rules impeded his wanderings except my one admonition to stay away from the pond. It was a more than small body of brackishness whose depths were unplumbed and whose edges were choked with every kind of snagging limb and cloying root imaginable. In fact, my one hesitation about moving back to country living had been taking children near that pond.

Surprisingly enough, however, for it is not the nature of little boys in general, John was perfectly willing to absent himself from the pond. It was Sam junior who, at five, was already the fisherman, the dreamer who needed only the faintest suggestion of a body of water to leave us entirely for the land of daydreams and imagination. As a result, it was Sam whom I watched with eagle eye and John to whom I gave the freedom of unmonitored movement. And move he did.

In the beginning he would come running home every five minutes to relate his most recent discovery and share the instant's most passionate adventure. As the newness settled down into something he could contain within himself, at least until dinnertime, he came in on a more hourly basis, mainly to be fed and watered.

By early July, of course, he had figured out that it was easier to get water from the outside spigots and food from the orchard than to bother with coming up to the house at all. There were, consequently, whole blocks of two or three hours when I did not see my son or receive any word from the battlefield. I had grown accustomed to such tranquillity when one morning, just before his long-anticipated birthday, he came bursting in.

I was in our upstairs bedroom making the bed and collecting the laundry when I heard the back door banged open and slammed hard against the sitting room wall. Before I could even yell down my "Don't let that door hit that wall one more time!" he was up the stairs and at my side, eyes big as saucers, his mouth wide open and wordless. He grasped his breath and my hand at the same moment. "Maw, Maw! You gotta come see!"

Without even bothering to ask, I hurried behind him, still connected by his grip on my hand, down the steps and to the kitchen window. "Look!" He was pointing toward the hen yard. "See that! Can you see that?"

All I could see was about seven or eight of Sam's hens and one very busy rooster. . . . One very busy rooster? Was that what he was so excited about?

"What am I supposed to see?" I asked him.

"That rooster . . . that rooster right there . . . is he doing what I think he's doing?"

"Yes"—my composure was incredible even to me—"Yes, I suspect that he is doing exactly what you think he is doing." 33

He dropped my hand slowly and stood watching, crossing his arms in front of him as though he were suddenly a thousand and five and wise beyond speaking in the ways of the world. Finally, shaking his head, he said, more or less to me, "Well, all I can say is I sure am glad I'm not a hen," and his leaving was much quieter than his entering had been.

He's seventeen now, still going on a thousand and five. A rooster himself, I suppose, if one cares to look at it that way. Certainly he's aware of the biological imperative that drives roosters and certainly he preens and crows enough to gratify even the most discriminating hens. What he's lost over the years since his poultry yard days, however, is the second part of his epiphany.

He's lost temporarily, as we all do, the naïveté that gives us a ready concern for our fellow creatures. He'll have to relearn it, of course, because he's neither rooster nor man, but Christian, a circumstance that requires him to.

He tried to challenge that the other night by laying on his father and me the bit about how we are all animals basically, flesh machines driven by appetites and responding to stimuli with only the faintest hope of any real control over our own actions. It was all straight out of the Seventeenth Chapter of the Book of Life, and neither parent bothered to refute it. If he had believed it, he wouldn't have been testing it out on us at the dinner table. Besides, we didn't have to. Rebecca did it for us.

"At least," she tossed out, "we can be taught to say thank you and animals can't. Not and mean it, that is."

Sam looked sharply down the table at me and said, "Hmmrump." John looked as startled as I have ever seen him. But Rebecca was oblivious to her own profundity. All she had meant was that she had passed me the peas as requested and then had been ignored in the intensity of the moment.

"Thank you," I said . . . and meant it.

4

The Day of
the Slaughter

Several years ago some parenting expert, probably Dr. Spock for all I know, amazed the nation by contending that one teaches one's children about sex by what one does, not by what one says. The same may also be said of religion, of course, though the truism, when applied to God, is less newsworthy by virtue of being less sensational. I discovered it, nonetheless, at the hands of another physician—my husband.

Originally it was a very simple thing, as most things are in their beginnings. It was the end of the first full calendar year of our being on the farm. Eighteen months, in other words, since we had come back to the busyness of garden produce and animal care. John was eight and a half by now and just beginning to understand that all this glory had to be paid for with the sweat of someone's brow. For the past year and a half, the sweat had come from his father's brow. Now some of it was beginning to come from his, and he was not sure he liked the change in our modus operandi too much.

Sam thought the time had come to return some of the excitement and novelty of the early days to John's life. Besides, the calves that he had bought almost two years before were now full-grown and ready to butcher. Once he had slaughtered our first beef, he said, we could truly say that we were self-sufficient on the land. Since that had been his goal all along, I was not sure how much of his motivation was John's well-being and how much was agrarian ambition. But it was a moot question, for we were going to slaughter a beef.

He and John roped Oscar, the most unlikely steer I have ever seen before or since (but one of the most delicious, I must add, though I could never understand how Sam knew that before the fact). Well, anyway, together they got a rope on Oscar and led him unprotesting to the stall in the barn which John had prepared for him. There, like an inmate on death row, Oscar had been enjoying the fat of the corn crib for almost a month.

The week after Christmas that year turned out to be the perfect one for Sam's purposes. The younger children were out of school, of course; his medical duties were light because no one who can help it gets sick over the holidays; and, to make things even more perfect, Mary was home from college. As if to add a final touch of sanction, the weather turned sharply cold on Monday afternoon—the kind of cold that lays a hard freeze on everything and doesn't let go, even in the middle of broad daylight.

On Wednesday afternoon when he came home from a short day at the office, Sam turned on the weather station and listened intently. Before dinner he watched the forecast on the television news. At supper he made his announcement. The weather was going to hold, and tomorrow we were going to butcher. A buzz of excitement went around the table with the hot biscuits. Kill a cow! How neat! Only Mary looked a bit anxious.

She was in her second year at the University of Maine. Because of the time and expense of traveling back and forth to Orono, she had spent all her holidays except Christmases with her roommates and friends—on their farms! She knew, she told me as we washed the dishes, that it was definitely time to worry.

She obviously had not spent her northern holidays in vain or conveyed her sympathies to me out of ignorance. Before I got up the next morning, she was already in the kitchen collecting all the big pots, scalding the meat grinder, covering the big table in newspaper and oilcloth, sharpening knives. She had been there.

Laura was horrified. "In here? He's going to cut it up in here?"

"We'll freeze to death out there. If you want to have any hands left, you'd better hope we do it in here."

"We! What's with this 'we' stuff? I don't intend to make hamburger this afternoon out of some steer who's eating his breakfast this morning."

"Great!" Mary was always a schemer, and I was beginning to get her drift, the reason for her early and portentous arranging of the utensils. "Then you can babysit Rebecca and Sam junior and also cook supper, while Mama and I do this." Neat kid, that girl. Crafty, but a good one to have on your side.

Laura gave it some consideration. Being bright, she knew she'd been outmaneuvered. The question was simply whether or not she minded. Since everyone was going to end up dog-tired before the day was over anyway, and since she would infinitely rather watch kids and make sandwiches than grind meat and freeze roasts, the only real loss was to her ego. She apparently decided against protesting and went instead to start on the beds.

Mary's predictions of the day were as accurate as her preparations had been. She and Sam took John with them as they went trudging off to the barn and the waiting Oscar. Rebecca observed for what was to be the first of many times that day that she really didn't think it was fair for John to go and her to not. "Later, Princess," was Sam's response to her as he shut the back door behind them.

Within five minutes I heard the shot, but no one else seemed to notice until John came popping like Father Christmas into the back door, eyes big and cheeks rosy. "Golly, Mom, he just dropped him right there in the stall. You shoulda seen how he did it. Dumb cow didn't know what happened. He and Mary are hoisting him up now. I gotta go watch 'em gut him," and he was gone again.

"Gag!" said Laura from behind me. "Don't men ever get tired of killing things?"

37

"I'm not sure this qualifies as killing things. We intend to eat him, you know."

"Sure it qualifies. It's just justified, is all. They're still getting the same bang out of it. Just look at that kid. He's excited to death because he got to see a cow shot."

"I still don't think it's fair that John gets to go," Rebecca butted in.

"Hush, baby," Laura Lee said absently, already paying little or no attention to Becca's complaint, and she set off toward the basement to start a load of laundry. "Well, I don't," was all I heard from Rebecca's retreating back as she docilely followed, leaving a trail of underwear and bath towels behind her.

The next hour was punctuated by John's enthusiastic messages from the back door, messages that always began, "Mom! Mom!" until I could get to the back door to receive the latest piece of intelligence.

"Mom, did you know Oscar made this big, huge cloud of steam when Dad cut him open?"

"Yes, son, I knew that."

"Wow!" and the door slammed shut again leaving me unsure of what had wowed him—the event or my information base.

"Mom! Mom!"

"Yes, John."

"Dad says I can have the horns if you say so and I saw 'em off."

"Right, son, but I think your brother may not like it."

"He's not out there working like I am. Fair's fair."

And then, reluctantly, "Mom! Dad says for me to bring Sam out for a little while. He wants to show us how the heart valves work, but he says it's too cold for Rebecca."

After the anatomy lesson was over (and I have to be honest and say that no child from here has ever failed an anatomy test, especially not one on the heart, lungs, or liver—a fact which is due, I am sure, directly to Sam's insistence on showing them at every slaughter exactly where muscles insert and blood vessels run and cusps shut) after the anatomy lesson was over, we progressed naturally, if not easily, into the business of the day and half the night.

The brains came in the door for Daddy's supper. I can't stand the things and never could, even as a child when my own father loved them. The liver was ushered in steaming by a disgruntled Mary, who opened the back door and hollered to no one in particular, "Take this thing!" and was gone again. I sliced and packaged liver while "Sesame Street" emanated from the family room and Laura washed blood off the back door.

"That's a waste of time if I ever saw one," I told her, but she was determined.

We had both finished before the first quarters hit the kitchen, carried this time by both Daddy and Mary, an ecstatic John tagging behind them. Sam moves swiftly when he's working and there was considerable grace in his cuts as he portioned and severed, sawed and boned. By four o'clock the quarters were rendered into steaks, roasts, and other. The other was going to take five more hours to be rendered into stew meat and hamburger.

Laura had been relegated to a very small but bloodless end of the kitchen from which she had faithfully been dispensing sandwiches and drinks for three hours already. Mary, with the bulk of the barn work done, sat down to begin the grinding; and I went on wrapping, marking, and freezing. We didn't see Sam again for a couple of hours except when he brought the ribs in to be severed and parceled. By dusk, however, he had finished the outside cleanup, washed the hide and put it in the tanning solution, and fed the stock. He came in the back door with the last of the pots for Laura to wash in the kitchen sink.

"Where's Becca?" he said.

"Pouting downstairs because she never even got to go out."

"Becca! Becca!" he called down the steps.

"What?" came an almost petulant, almost-five-years-old answer.

"Come see what I brought you from the barn," and he pulled a whitish looking piece of something from his pocket.

39

He got instant attention from the whole kitchen as well as from the family room.

Ever the showman, he insisted on waiting until Becca was upstairs before he took string out of the kitchen drawer and wound it tightly around one end of the flesh thing in his hand. Then, grinning—and so were Mary and I by now—he opened the bean sack and took out, very deliberately, three dried beans and dropped them into the other and open end of the thing in his hand. Sitting down in his accustomed chair and with Becca practically in his lap, he put the open end of the thing to his lips and began to blow. It expanded before her eyes, and they expanded before all of us. "What is it, Daddy? What is it? What is it?" over and over again, her insistence growing in direct proportion to Sam's unwillingness to quit blowing and talk.

Finally, when the thing had got as big as a basketball, Sam quit. He took it from his mouth, twisted the end and tied it as one ties a balloon. Handing it to her, he said, "Now feel it but be real easy with it until it dries." She did. He showed her how to rattle it and make the beans roll around merrily in it. "Now," he said after a few minutes of play, "we're going to hang it up here on this nail over the counter so it can dry. By tomorrow it will have turned almost clear and you can play with it." She was enthralled.

"But what is it?" said Laura.

"Oscar's bladder," Mary answered.

"His what?"

"His bladder," Mary repeated, plainly enjoying herself as much as Sam was.

"I had one every winter when I was little," he offered. "It was my favorite plaything."

"Oh, God!" said Laura.

But Rebecca was unmoved by it all as she pulled a chair over and began to gently bat the bladder back and forth on its nail.

With much less ado but with just as delighted a result, Sam took from his pocket four cleaned-out hooves, and Sam junior was quick to get the message. Now they each had a fair share of the day's goodies and each was content except for Rebecca's halfhearted protest that it was no fair the boys could take their parts to bed with them and hers had to stay hung up over the kitchen counter. Basically, however, she was too tired to really care and Laura was too disgusted to give her much slack. So the young ones were bedded down finally, and the old ones sat up till almost midnight grinding. The day was done and we were "self-sufficient on the land" at last.

As a sequence of events, we would repeat the process many times before we got to be few enough and old enough to no longer need to kill our own beef. The boys, during those years, took turns over who got the horns and who got the hooves, but Becca always ended up with the bladder.

The horns and hooves would turn up from time to time in various interesting and arresting uses. They were turned into the predictable powder horns and carved into the predictable boxes and handles. One year the best jack-o'-lantern we ever had sported a pair of somebody's horns above a mean, Brunhilde kind of face. But the bladder always stayed hung on the nail above the kitchen counter when it was not being played with. Though it changed from year to year and sometimes broke before its replacement arrived, it was the only ball in our history that was always faithfully returned to its place after every use.

Our friends and intimates got used to seeing it there, just as they probably got used to jack-o'-lanterns with real horns. Most of the adults, in fact, would take it down and play with it themselves as they stood in the kitchen talking and visiting while I cooked our meal or cleaned up one we had just shared. By the very nature of things, of course, most of those familiar friends were writers or editors or publishers, folks who could accept a cow's bladder with more grace than most. One in particular, however, was important to me.

She was a longtime and dear friend, almost fifteen years my junior and still at the start of her career the first time she pulled the bladder off its nail, and asked, "What's this?"

"Oscar's bladder," Rebecca answered.

"I thought so. I haven't had one in years," Lynne responded, turning it over to make the beans roll and rattle.

The next time she came to visit, it was Covenant's bladder

41

hanging on the nail and she rolled it in her hands more thoughtfully than she had the previous one.

"What's up?" I asked her.

"The boys do anything bizarre with Covenant's horns and hooves?"

"No, they had to split the hooves this year because Covie didn't have horns."

"Oh." She was still propped against the counter, moving the ball in her hands and thinking.

"Penny for your thoughts."

"Not worth a penny," she said. "At least not yet."

"What're you working on?"

"A piece I really want to do . . . have ever since I picked up Oscar's bladder last winter . . . on death. I see it everywhere I go in town. And when I'm on the road! Lord, you wouldn't believe the number of dead animals you see in the middle of the road these days!" She shook her head as if to clear what was in it. Then she tried again. "When I'm out here, it seems so easy. The kids are so unconcerned with it. They play with bladders and hooves and horns and eat meat and pluck chickens and watch Sam shoot coons and it doesn't bother any of you."

"Come on, you grew up this way. You remember how it is on a farm. There's always more life than the land can support!" I was a little disconcerted, I suppose, by the unexpected direction our evening was taking. "You kill part of it to eat. You kill part of it to keep it from killing you, literally or figuratively. Nature kills the rest, either before or after it reproduces itself. We're built on death here or anywhere else. There's just no concrete or pretense out here to hide it."

"Only a Christian could say that," she responded.

"Say what?"

"Say we're built on death."

"No," I said, "any realist could say that. And any religious man could say that we should value the death we're built on. And any moralist could say that there's a difference in sentient death and non-sentient, with human obligation falling on us to relieve the former rather than the latter, and so forth and so on." I was disgusted, faintly but definitely, by this brand of quasi-effeteness, especially in a woman who was neither an intellectual dullard nor an emotional patsy.

"And what would any Christian say?" she pushed on, ignoring my testiness.

"Beats me," I said finally, being unable, much to my chagrin, to come up with even the feeblest answer to her question.

"Maybe I'll ask Sam why he thinks it's important to give the kids these things every time he butchers." She was ruminating more to herself than to me, and I forgot about the conversation until two nights later.

It was her last night with us on this visit before going back to her apartment in the big city and her next assignment. We were in the kitchen again, just after supper, and I was still loading the dishwasher when she took down the ball and began to rotate it in her two hands.

"Did you ask Sam?"

"Yeah," she grinned.

"Well," I said. "What did he say?"

"What I should have known without asking."

"Which was . . . ?"

"Which was that he gives the stuff to them so they can have fun."

"That's all?"

"No. He also said he gives it to them so they won't take themselves too seriously."

Well, she was right about one thing. I can't say that about just any Christian, but both of us certainly should have known what mine would say.

5

In the Company
of Good Cats

Y ou don't have to be one of the Parker Brothers to figure out that games simulate life, that to be successful as games they must allow us experience with impunity. Much the same thing can be said about pets, especially about domestic ones; they become surrogate people and surrogate experience with at least some impunity. I have always treasured ours for that reason, especially our cats.

We have a tomcat—doesn't everyone!—and he is so straight out of that Morris-the-Cat tradition of red-headed good looks and polished virility that we long ago gave up calling him anything except Morris . . . which, of course, is not really fair to him. The fact that one is the epitome of a type should never be allowed to blur the more potent fact that one is an individual, certainly not with cats.

And we have had a progression of cats. I honestly don't know why. As a child, I was deathly allergic to them. But in all the world, they were my most favorite animal even then, and I can remember sitting for hours in my bedroom stroking one cat or another while the tears ran down my cheeks and something less acceptable ran out of my nose. The waterworks was worth it, though, so long as I could play with a cat.

I suppose in time my parents gave up on denying me access to the cats and decided to just let my respective orifices run.

Miraculously enough, the minute I put the cat of the moment down, my watering stopped with no apparent residual. I have always been extraordinarily grateful.

The first cat I can remember by name with any intimacy was named Patsy, which was interesting since he sported as fine and obvious a set of equipment as any tomcat ever has; but that was of less concern to me in those days of childhood.

Patsy lived with us in the years at Ritter Hall when I was three and four and going on obnoxious. Being in an all-adult world is tough on a cat; having a three-year-old owner who has been reared in an all-adult world is tougher. I thought I knew almost everything (it has been a difficult position for me to relinquish over the five decades since), and no one was to ever understand that more clearly than Patsy.

As our family finances improved in step with the nation's recovering, post-depression economy and with my father's rising academic status, we began to enjoy certain amenities that had not previously been part of our lives or anyone else's in the first half of the thirties.

The first luxury that I was truly aware of at any level of wonder was a vacuum cleaner. The word was put out at supper one night, tentatively but prayerfully, that Mr. Fees, the local barber and Electrolux dealer in our college town, had asked for an appointment to come demonstrate the brand-new, 1938 models right there in our own apartment. And, my mother allowed hesitantly, she had told him she would be delighted to have him stop by the next day so long as he understood that there was no possibility of our buying just at this time.

When nothing happened at the other end of our small supper table—when not even a facial muscle moved at the paternal end—I figured, correctly, that we were about to get our first vacuum cleaner. Even at not quite four, I wasn't too young to know that.

My mother apparently figured the same way I did because the next afternoon she was asking very specific questions the way one does about a piece of equipment one fully intends to activate to its entire potential.

"Yes, you can wash the bag and cut down on the wear, but it

would be better, Mrs. Alexander, if you could see your way clear to budget in a new bag at least once a year." (Some of the ladies had tried to mend their bags because they had rinsed them too frequently and worn them out that way, but a mended bag was not a safe bag. "It allows particulate matter to escape into the machine, you understand.")

I understood that particulate matter was very significant and probably the biggest two words Mr. Fees had at his command. That much I understood.

"Now, as for the animal problem with the baby's allergies . . ."

"What baby?" I wanted to know. I also wanted to stomp on Mr. Fees' big fat foot, but I couldn't. My mother would have killed me, and besides, by this point in the afternoon, I was really lusting after that glorious twenty-two-inches-on-chrome-runners of power and noise and bulbous classiness. I wanted that machine—for what I didn't know—but the pride of near-ownership was already ablaze in my heart.

"So, Mrs. Alexander, it is perfect for cleaning cat hair up. All you do is turn the floor tool over like this—see these rounded teeth here?—they drop down when you turn the tool over and they just gently lift the hair right up without hurting a thing."

Some other question must have ensued about the other uses of the machine because the next thing I knew my mother was connecting the hose to the back end of the machine and, under Mr. Fees' tutelage, demonstrating to herself how she could dry my hair in the blast of hot air that the thing expelled from its rear. For the first time I could see certain parts of this that were less than appealing (and remained so for all the years that my mother blew my hair dry in what can only be remembered as a controlled riptide of a gale), but my covetousness exceeded my wisdom.

I was overjoyed when finally, two pot roasts, an angel food cake, and three messes of fried chicken later, my father in the following week agreed to sign the contract that made the Electrolux ours. What I had not foreseen, in my almost-four naïveté, was that once the thing was ours, it was really my mother's and not ours at all—certainly not mine.

46

I chewed on that fact for what must have been days, but that I remember as having been months. I wanted desperately to run, to control, to govern that enormous power and that substantial noise. Mother would have none of it. The Electrolux was new; it was expensive; it was hers . . .

. . . until one day when one of those fearsome and anxiety-provoking receptions was upon us. Although the young women from the School of Home Economics (that's honestly what they called it, folks) always came over to prepare and serve the dreadful things as part of their coursework, my mother was supposed to be there at all times to instruct, also part of their coursework. She also told my father rather frequently that even if she weren't required by the college to be with them every minute, she still would have to hover in order to keep them from destroying every dish and bowl she owned.

Anyway, one of those things was going to happen in the afternoon, and my mother was engrossed in domestic defense policies as a result. Left to my own devices and with all my collegiate playmates in morning classes, I arrived for the first time in my life at an understanding of the term *carpe diem*. To outright defy my mother was never smart, but to outmaneuver her was frequently possible.

The reasoning, the best I can reconstruct it, must have gone something like: if one is engaged in a beneficial or kindly intended act and if one is clever, one can often get away with the forbidden by showing it to have been an essential ingredient of the proposed beneficial and kindly intention. Having secured the premise, I proceeded with its application.

I assembled the new vacuum in the middle of my room in just the way I had watched Mr. Fees and Mother do, being sure that the hose was attached to the sucking and not the ejecting end of things. Then I plugged in the cord without incident and turned the floor tool over so those gently rounded teeth protruded. Next I went to find Patsy. If anything would endear me to my mother and excuse me for having used the new vacuum, certainly cleaning the cat would—or that was my thinking on the matter.

Cat in hand, I sat back down on the linoleum rug of my

47

bedroom, positioned the purring Patsy firmly between my outstretched legs, set the inverted tool squarely on top of Patsy's back, and turned on the switch. What happened next is a little unclear to me now and probably was then.

Somehow, in a space of time that seemed instantaneous but couldn't have been, the room was full of noise—some feline, some mechanical, some pediatric, and some maternal. Mother was screaming bloody corruption at some nonsensical and noncommunicative level; I was enraged over the pain in my scratched and bloody legs; and the poor Electrolux was gasping for air around a baseball-size wad of hair.

Some nice young lady from the College of Home Economics unplugged the vacuum, although I suspect she never married and ran one of her own afterwards. My mother calmed down to being merely hysterical, and my father, that night, repaired the hole in the screen where Patsy had vaulted straight through the open window without stopping for the screen.

Three nights later, a defaced and permanently insecure Patsy came home, his reversed Mohican haircut no longer bloody, but with his head definitely bowed. Ever after that, our first chore in cleaning house was to find and evict Patsy before flipping the switch on the vacuum. On the three different occasions when one or the other of us forgot, my father lost, respectively, two more window screens and one glass door pane as a result.

Patsy moved with us from Ritter Hall to the new old house off campus, but he never lost his Pavlovian training. He died, in fact, during the post–World War II days when Piper Cubs were first new and plentiful in our town. The similarity of their motor sounds to those of an oversized vacuum cleaner was just too much for old Patsy, and his heart couldn't take being kick-started five or six times a day every day of the week. I loved him dearly and used him, in the main, wisely, but I never flip on a vacuum cleaner of any brand without remembering him.

Patsy's life with us had been so traumatic that my parents would never risk replacing him with another cat. Instead they moved to dogs and I moved to marriage, there being a difference of sorts between the two.

Actually my return to the business of cats did not occur until Sam and I had completed all of our respective schooling and had settled down to earning a living and raising babies. By that time Patsy had been dead for well over ten years and we had moved nine times in the pursuit of Sam's medical degree, my master's, his internship, a residency, my fellowship, his fellowship, his appointment to the medical faculty at the university, and finally his practice. To put it mildly, I was very, very ready at that stage of our lives for a cat and for the stability that cats, God bless 'em, always create in life.

But, as if in compensation for the long interruption in our stability, our first Tickle cat turned out to be two cats, an unexpected but matched set, so to speak.

The Greek professor at the college where I was lecturing at the time, Dr. Ben Cook, to be exact, somewhat suddenly and without much lead time, received an invitation from our government to join an international team of classicists and archaeologists on summer digs in the Aegean Islands. Ben, who was flattered, and his wife, who was frantic, had two Siamese cats that they obviously (we're back to felines' penchant for stability again) could not take with them on some kind of floating College of the Aegean. Would we take them for the summer? Would we! I was ecstatic . . . until Ben told me that the cats only spoke Greek.

It had been quite a while since I had struggled through my last Greek class and I certainly had never spoken it. But I shouldn't have worried. Even if I didn't speak Greek, Sam spoke a highly accomplished patois of Cat, a facility that I had previously been unaware of in him.

Si (the other one was named Am, of course; this was in the days when *The Lady and the Tramp* was big box office) was pregnant at the time the two joined us—it was something of a habit with her, we were to discover—and her pregnancy may have hastened her familiarity with Sam along a bit. Whatever the cause, she immediately took upon herself the role of new daughter, most needy patient, and benevolent nuisance.

They talked by the hour in the strangest noises I had ever

49

heard. To see a grown man, a physician even, cock his head and, out of the side of his mouth, emit a well-rounded, moaning howl that rises as his head turns to crescendo and dies on the other side of his face is rather shattering. The only thing worse is when a cat answers him in what is obviously a meaningful response. Am and I—she at least was reasonable, thank goodness—were cut completely out of Si and Sam's relationship.

Then came the day that Sam set the doors to the liquor closet ajar one morning and told me to leave them open. "Why?" seemed a reasonable question. We had had nothing but trouble with Si, ever since her coming, over that liquor closet. She loved getting in there at every opportunity and making the bottles tinkle and clack. She had already spilled one bottle of bitters by turning it over and had exploded another (full to very top with soda water, in fact) by the same method. I had had it with Si and the liquor closet.

"Because," Sam said with impervious calm and before I could object, "she's going to deliver and that's where she wants to be."

"*Wants* to be?"

"Will be most comfortable," he amended, lest I embarrass him with some direct questions.

Sure enough, before supper that night, I heard the bottles tinkling and clacking, and Sam had his kittens.

The bottles tinkled and clacked many a time after that at our house—the woman had no morals at all—but the Cooks, long since returned from the Aegean, refused to take Si and Am back. Actually, I think Sam rather dared them to try, and Ben, a very sober and scholarly fellow, told me in all seriousness that he would never interrupt a Siamese relationship like Si's with Sam. "It's most unusual," he said confidentially. I certainly couldn't argue with that, and Si and Am lived out the rest of their days with us, both dying of old age shortly before we sold the house and moved to the farm.

Because Si was Sam's and Am was nobody's—a much nobler tradition in cats, may I say—I and the children, as they had come along, had been forced to take on other cats for ourselves. And there has been a motley crew of them over the years.

Ones, for instance, like Sargeant, who was the only tired cat I ever knew. He was, in fact, a tired kitten before he became a tired cat. From the very first, we had to feed Sargeant carefully—stand there even and see that he ate—a process which Nora used to complain of bitterly when she was little and it was her job. But unless someone watched Sargeant, he would fall asleep in front of the cat dish and, even after falling face down into his own food, forget what it was he was there to do.

We used to have dozens of pictures of Sargeant asleep in the sunshine with a sparrow or a pigeon standing beside him and staring, head cocked in disbelief, at the phenomenon dozing there. My favorite shot, however, was the one of Sargeant sleeping on the wall of the patio with a sparrow resting just as peacefully on his back—but that only happened once.

Then I certainly can't forget Sunshine. She was, as her name would suggest, a delightful and seductive strawberry blonde, who, like Si and Am, had an academic heritage. Actually, she came to us by way of the college cafeteria and three undergraduates in my freshman advisory group who could not bear to see her homeless. Having tried to keep her hidden from the housemother in their dorm closets and having failed, they appealed to us for relief. Sam agreed and Sunshine came home with me one afternoon from the campus.

Accustomed to lots of people and to dorm life, she fit right in with us except that she had not learned the skills of dodging human feet. After supper, on her very first night with us, Sam strapped then baby John on his back and took Laura Lee's hand to go for a walk in the evening twilight. On his way out, he also picked up the garbage (in order to save me a trip out later) and Nora and Mary, who suddenly decided to go too. So Daddy headed out, baby on his back, garbage on his front, one little girl by the hand, two more loose on each side, and absolutely no visibility.

Just as he put his foot firmly down to knee open the back porch screen, we both heard it. There was no meow, no cry, 51 only the scrunch of breaking bones. Neither John, too little, nor Laura, too innocent, nor Mary and Nora, too loud, had heard it. Sam looked at me and shook his head.

Walking on out the door, he turned and said, "Come on, Mama. You take these children for a walk. I just remembered I have to do something." And he motioned me onto the patio where he gave me Laura's hand and strapped John off his back and onto mine. In my ear he whispered: "Take at least twenty minutes. I'm sure it's dead, but I'll have to find some place to bury it." I nodded and headed out to the street while the unsuspecting children waved to their father as he headed in the opposite direction to the alley with our garbage.

Half an hour later and half dead from carrying both John and Laura the last two blocks, I came dragging home to a kitchen that looked more like an orthopedic suite than the room I had left. There on a kitchen table now cleared of all its usual appointments was an open shoe box. From both of its longer sides emerged two tongue depressors, which had obviously been bradded firmly in place with considerable precision. They were as rigid as they were straight. From the top of each depressor and secured by having been passed through a hole in their tops was a complicated series of rubber bands looped together and controlled in the middle by a kind of tension device fashioned from paper clips. The rubber bands terminated, each of them, in a hind foot, which terminated in Sunshine.

I looked in absolute disbelief at the tiny cat lying flat on its back, feet tied up in the air and hind legs in traction. Under her, Sam had spread a padding of old rags, and to each side he had packed beside her a restraining but soft bumper of more rags. He had shaved her lower quarters before he had taped her into the rubber bands and had sedated her with some kind of injection. The razor—mine, I might add—the needle, the leftover rags, the evicted pair of my Sunday shoes, and some assorted desk supplies lay on the table as mute testimony to what he had been doing while I was walking. He shrugged when I looked as if I were about to ask. "She wasn't dead after all, just got both legs broken," he said.

"Can she live like that?"

"We'll see," he answered. "Orthopedics isn't my strong suit and veterinary science sure as hell isn't, but she deserves a chance," and he proceeded to cut the first of several dozen diapers for her. Before the evening was over, he had also gotten Laura's doll bottle and fed Sunshine her first supine snack.

Over the next few weeks we changed diapers and fed bottles and carried the shoe box out for fresh air and in for warmth with as much care as if that cat had been the Queen of England. Near the end, Sam would feel every night or two along the back legs, sometimes adjusting the tension in his traction machine, sometimes not doing anything except scratching Sunshine's chest for her.

The afternoon eventually came when I saw him get out the scissors from his bag and I knew he was about to cut her free. That she had lived at all was a miracle. That she might indeed ever walk again seemed unthinkable. I suppose I had never really thought beyond Sunshine in the shoe box, never given any belief to what it would mean if she should recover. But Sam is ever the healer, ever the believer.

He released the rubber bands and snipped away the adhesive tape anchors that had held them. He took away the bumpers and turned Sunshine belly side down for the first time in almost seven weeks. She meowed and cried, but she made no effort to move. We left her there and went to bed.

The next morning she was still in the box and Sam set her out on the back porch floor with a bowl of food and another of water beside her. That afternoon when he came home, she was right where he had left her and he sighed heavily before he finally sat down on the porch floor a good three or four feet from her and began to croon "Here, Kitty, Kitty. Come on, Sunshine. Come on, Baby. Come on." He wiggled his fingers and tapped the floor and traced imaginary designs with a straw out of my broom, but nothing happened other than Sunshine's moving her head as the straw moved and meowing as Sam called. Nothing.

We were eating supper when we all heard her claws scraping the wooden floor of the back porch. Sunshine was trying to stand up! And stand up she did before the night was over.

53

It was several days before she could get into the litter box and Sam felt safe in taking off her diapers. It was even longer, of course, before her head didn't look as if it were going forty-five degrees to the right of where her hind quarters were going, but she walked and eventually she played and then ran and climbed and, within three months, did everything that any other almost grown kitten could do . . . except that for the rest of her days she slept on her back.

We would find her propped beside a wall or a tree or a step for support, all four feet straight up in front of her and snoring away. After awhile the children and I quit trying to explain her to relatives and friends and took to saying, "Oh, it's a long story. You don't want to know about it." But Sam, who always regarded her cure as one of his most noteworthy achievements in medicine, will still proceed to explain every detail of Sunshine's remarkable progress and eventual recovery to anyone foolish enough to ask him.

Of all our city cats, however, Sir Thomas Le Chat and not Sunshine was my favorite, which is to say that he was the one of all of them who had the wisdom to most prefer my company to that of the children or Sam or even of the other cats.

Sir Thomas was the most elusively blue and gray I have ever seen. He was a big cat, but perfectly proportioned, and he was pathologically obsessed with his remarkable body. (I would have been too, if I had ever been that lucky!) He spent most of his life on top of the refrigerator from whose height and position of grandeur he could properly command my attention while he groomed and re-groomed his luminous fur. But that was in the city where the living was easy. It was not until we moved to the farm that Sir Thomas Le Chat rose to his full stature as a man.

In the first month of our new life, Sir Thomas wore himself almost into leanness trying to get himself settled in. He was particularly occupied with getting his boundaries established. I spent more than one morning watching him move from orchard tree to orchard tree delivering his potent message of ownership to all the other tomcats who might get any ideas about this newcomer, this city cat with city ways. Let there be no question that a gentleman, though bred in the city, could fight as clean a battle and earn as definitive a victory as any country hick of a cat.

So Sir Thomas, he who had previously sprayed only my furniture and won only my wrath, now sprayed uncounted fence posts and innumerable trees before he felt free to doze on his new patio . . . much less to wander off and test some other cat's borders.

The children laughed about poor Thomas and his exhausted spraying machine, but his earnestness was only half-funny. I understood, or at least I thought I did, his need to buy his space for himself. Wandering the pastures in the afternoons before Sam would come home for supper or walking the fence lines with him to find where a calf had gotten out or even sitting quietly at my typewriter trying to catch and hold all of this new world before it could grow familiar, I was doing the same thing. We were laying claim, Sir Thomas and I, to new territory, which, since it was country territory, required country ways. But that was all that either of us had done or was doing.

As for Sir Thomas nowadays, he has long since ceased to acknowledge our position of sole ownership. Some time back he found a four-legged lady whom he likes better than me. We see him from time to time still when he saunters in to the patio just to check us out and be sure that we are still as we should be. He never stays long and he scarcely deigns to eat our fare; he has grown more accustomed now to squirrel and sparrow and mouse, I suppose.

But he is somehow more regal than he was. Leaner, more powerful, quicker. If his coat is not quite so well groomed as it used to be, at least I see it frequently repeated in kittens and maturing cats around the village and on neighboring farms. He's a busy cat, a good cat, who makes me believe in the truth of Robin Hood. It is no small gift, I tell him, on those rare occasions when he still lets me hold him in my lap.

But that gets us back to Morris, who is the current lord of the manor. How long he will hold his position, I can't say. Scurvy (ugliest cat I ever saw, but one of the dearest) and Alouette (the harlot of the group, as you would surmise) both have new litters, some of which are bound to be toms. In about nine or ten months, Morris will yet once again have to prove his mettle or be pushed on to some other feeding dish. In the meanwhile, he commands the patio and the loyalty of the ladies.

When Sir Thomas comes calling, it is a meeting of gentlemen and no swords are drawn. I hope it will continue to remain so, for I am fond of them both and old enough to think new toms should find new territory and leave us older folks alone at last. (John and Sam junior both see that issue a bit differently.) We will see how it all plays down.

In the meanwhile, and for at least six more months, we have a peaceful patio and a peaceful feline world which, even if its population shifts, will continue, as it always has, to reverence only one thing, namely its own catness. Such integrity, of course, is the reason that cats have often been regarded, by cultures less skittish than ours, as divine.

I think of that a lot these days as I watch the new and what must be, for this family, two hundredth generation of kittens growing fat and saucy on the patio. Perhaps the most significant and least celebrated benefit of living with animals of any kind is that one can see many, many generations of them in the course of one's own single, human experience. Such watching gives, if nothing else, an appreciation for inviolate pattern. In cats, it also gives humor and belief in the goodness of process. Since I can't climb out of our lives and sit on top of them like Sir Thomas on the refrigerator, I can at least be thankful for the chance to sit watchfully on top of theirs. It is a gift which, like believing in Robin Hood and heroes, tends ultimately to draw one to prayer and to shame one finally into faith.

6

The Bleeding Birds

Not all the creatures in our lives have been subject to domestication, of course. Some of those most central to our experience have also been the wildest, like the egrets, for instance.

We first saw the birds—we think—in the fall of 1978. There's no way now to be sure, of course. Back then we didn't record the farm's naturally occurring fauna with the same care that we used to track the equipment and the stock. I wish we had. But at the time we thought they were just cranes that had, for some unknown reason, come farther inland than usual from the Mississippi.

Mary saw them first and came running. I was upstairs moving winter clothes (the reason I know it was fall, in fact) out of the hall closet and getting ready to carry them out to the back clotheslines to air when she came charging up the stairs saying, "This you won't believe!" and went beyond me toward our bedroom and her father's binoculars.

Actually, they were Sam's only in name and in placement. They had once been one of his proudest—and most expensive, I must add—possessions. That was in the city. They had also been one of the few things unequivocally denied to children and usually to spouse. They were Daddy's. That, as I say, had been in the city.

Country living, with its myriad excitements and thousand **57** wonders, had eroded Sam's proprietary position down to having the things still referred to as "Daddy's binoculars" and to a firm rule that, when not in use, they were always to hang in their case, closed preferably, from the large loop of his tie rack securely shut within the confines of his closet. He frequently and bitterly mentioned to me that all that this had accomplished was to remind him of the days when he had once been in control . . . that, and keeping his ties in an eternal jumble.

But while he was away fighting bacteria and neuroses, I was left on the homefront; and riding shotgun on his binoculars, much less his ties, had just simply been beyond me. Consequently the children, especially the older ones like Mary who were essentially grown, had long since given up even saying what they were doing as they headed toward their father's tie rack.

When she emerged from our bedroom, therefore, I knew without looking what Mary had gone in for and what she had come out with. I met her, as a result, in our bathroom.

Our bathroom, long since a failure as a bathroom but a huge success as a family room (a private bath is the only part of retirement that I am looking forward to with real enthusiasm), enjoys, among its other questionable assets, an absolutely unequaled view of the back ten acres of the Lucy Goosey. Why, I have never figured out.

I have, from time to time, accused the original builder/owner of a perverse sense of human function, but the widest vista in north Shelby County can still be had from our bathroom. Even the smaller children and now the grandson insist that standing on the lowered lid of the commode in our bathroom provides them with the "grandest look in the whole world," a regrettable truth unless one really likes scrubbing the upside of one's commode a lot. But that has nothing to do with the birds; Mary does and did.

As I was saying, I headed to our bathroom when I saw her go toward our bedroom, and we met at the commode and the window above it. She was right. It didn't even take Sam's glasses for me to know what she had seen and to agree that no one was ever going to believe it.

The whole back pasture from the fence line halfway to the cattle pond was white with them. And they were moving as the sea moves, in undulation and curve and lift and fall. Never had I seen such a thing. The sheer magnificence of their whitecaps on our stubbled hay was beyond my capacity to react to. I stood stunned into silence by the sensuousness of their movement. Nobody said anything in the bathroom for a full minute and a half, maybe two, before I understood that the children also had to see. "Call them to come quietly," I whispered to Mary, and she nodded and went.

They came—loudly until they saw—and then they too stood silently as they gathered, one by one, in front of the window. The pasture beyond us continued to roll and rise, lift and resettle.

"May we go out to them?" It was John, understandably, who was so hushed by what he was watching. At eight he was the one least likely to be quiet, much less to speak with precision. Looking down at him, however, I realized that he needed to move out and into the birds.

"Yes," I answered him back as softly as he had asked.

But while the rest of us watched, the birds, as if sensing his approach, lifted one last time, hundreds of them, and moved westward before the boy even got downstairs, much less out of the house.

The next time they came, there were fewer of them and it was almost winter. The wools and corduroys had not only been aired and hung into our respective closets; they were being worn again. We watched the birds with just as much excitement, perhaps, but with a great deal more skill.

The second time it was Laura and John and I who stood in the bathroom and watched. The birds showed less restiveness, and we dared, all three of us, to open the back door and go out toward them. We eventually made it to the fence without alarming them, and we stood watching for maybe a quarter of an hour before even that happened. But in that quarter of an hour we could see and share with each other enough of their features to realize that whatever they were, they weren't cranes.

It would be almost three years later, when the birds had

59

become a three-or-four-times-every-fall part of our lives, that John, still absorbed by the meaning of them, would finally come home with proof of their identity. They were cattle egrets. *Scientific American* or *National Geographic* or *Smithsonian* or some similar publication, I can't remember exactly which now, said so.

He brought the magazine home and laid it open in front of me on the kitchen counter when he came in from school one day. "Look what I found," he insisted, and there, in the current issue of whatever, were our birds, along with a six- or seven-page essay about the miracle of their arrival in North America.

The cattle egret is indigenous to Africa, where it has apparently lived for centuries. For some reasons unknown to the *Smithsonian* or whoever, the birds had begun in the 1930s to migrate. They had made it into the Mississippi Valley, the article said, in 1977.

The whole paper was basically about the miracle of the birds' transoceanic travel and of the newness of their time with us. Reading John's magazine, I was awfully glad that we had had the birds for several seasons before we had had the footnotes that explained and validated them. Miracles, in general, suffer a certain loss of poetry when they become certifiable. The children seemed to agree with me, although I suppose in fairness to science I ought to confess that it was nice to know what the birds really were, and it was rather intellectually exhilarating to know we had a world-class miracle, or at least a media event, in our pasture.

But the birds, either because of the consistency of their fall appearances or because of the article or because of that demon, familiarity, became less important, less startling, over the years of the early eighties.

Then it was April, 1985. This time we are all sure of when it was because we had grown more careful of our details and more proprietary toward our miracles. I was sitting at the kitchen table paying bills when, for some reason, probably fiscal distress, I turned around in my chair and looked out the picture window behind me toward the pasture. There, high in the dead oak that stands in a small close at the upper end of the pasture, was a wounded egret.

His breast was covered in blood and he appeared to be too weary or weak to do anything except cling to his perch in silence. He was, even in his distress, incredibly arresting, more breathtaking, in fact, than I could remember the birds ever having been in the past. I could not decide whether it was the April light, the singleness of this one bird alone, or the abnormally heightened yellow of his comb that accounted for his great beauty, but passionately beautiful he was.

It was already mid-afternoon, and I quietly put my work away and gave myself up entirely to watching the injured egret. He moved not at all. He did nothing. Unlike the usual pattern of lifting and resettling that the birds had always followed before, this one either couldn't or wouldn't move, much less fly. He simply hung there high in the dead oak.

In a few minutes, another egret flew in and settled wearily down on an adjacent limb. He too had been injured. He too was bleeding through his breast feathers. Enemies? I wondered. Mating rivals who had fought earlier in the day and had met here to complete their contest? If so, neither seemed to have the strength or the will to continue their battle. I began to wish for the children to come home.

Just before three o'clock the first school bus pulled up, and one by one we became a family again. Beyond us in the pasture the egrets began to assemble also. By three-thirty there were seven of them in the old oak, each one of them incredibly commanding in its beauty, each one possessed of a brilliant yellow comb, each one bleeding across the whole of its chest and lower body. None of them was moving.

Either these were birds who fought in a very consistent and destructive manner, or something else was happening here. I theorized out loud that even ritual fighting would allow some variation in the wound sites. And fighting to the point of such bloody results seemed incompatible with the kind of longevity and strength it takes to migrate from one continent across a major ocean to another continent. We all agreed that the whole thing didn't make sense.

Finally, I did what now seems to have been the logical 61

thing, but which at the time seemed almost silly. I picked up the phone and called the municipal zoo in the city and asked for the ornithologist on staff. The ornithologist on staff, whoever the poor soul may have been, was plainly not accustomed to getting calls in the middle of the afternoon from John Q. Public, especially not from Mrs. John Q. Public. "You have what?" he asked me again.

"I have a tree full of wounded egrets," I repeated.

He started laughing. "M'am, do those egrets have red breasts, yellow combs, and acute weariness?"

"Yes, sir, that's exactly what they have."

"What they also have is a high level of hormones," he chuckled. "It's springtime, Lady, even in birdland," and he sounded like he was going to hang up.

"Wait! Can you tell me what they're doing?" (Stupid question, I realized, and started over.) "I mean, have they been fighting?"

That seemed to be a more manageable question, and my authority audibly relaxed. "No, m'am. They actually don't seem to fight at all. The males just grow that comb and their chests turn red and then they sit somewhere while the females choose which mate they want, like a high school prom for us, only in reverse."

"Well, they surely look like they're bleeding to death."

"Can you imagine a more appropriate way to go? Blood first, before the sweat and tears." He was chuckling again.

"No, sir, I guess I can't," I said and, thanking him, hung up.

That night when all the excitement had died down and when each of us had relayed to Daddy his or her own rendition of the bleeding birds, I repeated for Sam my conversation with the ornithologist, including his crack about the appropriateness of blood, sweat, and tears.

"Forget the sweat and tears," Sam responded sleepily from his side of the evening paper. "They're part of getting up every morning. It's the blood that seals the deal."

"Oh, you think so, do you!" I was prepared, despite the sleepy voice, to engage in a sharp discussion in defense of marriage as a pretty good thing.

"Baby," he said, lowering the paper briefly, "everything we

do in this life that we know, deep down in our guts, we can't ever undo, we mark with blood or holy water or both. If you aren't old enough to know that yet, at least those birds are"—which, it occurred to me as he retreated back behind his paper, was as good a definition of the difference between the sacred and the profane as I had ever heard . . . as well as of the bittersweet holiness of mating.

CONCRETE
ABSTRACTIONS

——— 7 ———

Just as We Are

There are, I have discovered over the years, as many ways to write a book as there are ways to prepare an apple or settle a fuss. The possibilities are limitless in all three activities. King Solomon was probably never more correct in his life than he was when he noted that "of the making of many books, there is no end." He could also have added that there is no method either.

Over the years of pursuing any activity, however, including the making of many books (thirteen, and articles and columns and essays), one begins to develop certain tricks or devices or points of view or just plain favorite subject matter for the telling of tales. Professionally speaking, this is an entirely defensible phenomenon, a desirable one, in fact, if one is to ever get on with the work of tale-telling. The only place it seems to go awry is for those on whom the tales are told. I was first made aware of this one night last winter.

It was in early November, when school had been going long enough that we all were tired unto death of 6:30 A.M. school buses and after-school-until-dark track meets. It looked from where we stood as if the Thanksgiving holiday would definitely never come, and even if it did, it would definitely be too brief and too busy to relieve the wearies of either our bodies or our psyches.

Sam, who will deny it, always gets really tedious in the late fall. The kids used to call it "Daddy's Winter Psychosis." I just call it Sam-in-the-cold. He can't bear having to stay inside, and he cannot tolerate not having things growing everywhere all the time. I've more than a few times thought that that was probably why we have all these children—they are kind of his guarantee of a year-round crop. But there's a limit to how many of them one can afford, as we eventually figured out; so Sam-in-the-cold has just had to settle for being annoyed that winter is going to come every year and stay for four months at least, whether he likes it or not. And he doesn't like it, which, as I was saying, was part of the trouble, along with the school blahs, last November.

It was after supper, but I was still in the kitchen, dawdling more than working. Nights are my favorite time, anyway. (Mothers usually are allowed to dawdle after the last meal of the day has been prepared, fed, and removed.) Actually I was dawdling over cleaning up the stove. I honestly like to clean the stove. More correctly, I like turning off all the kitchen lights except the fluorescent over the sink and then seeing, all around me, shiny and satiny, the polished stove top and the counters glistening in its glow. It makes me feel as if I have a leg up on the next day if the kitchen is shut down and pristine. So I was putting the last strokes of affection on the stove top when the rumbles broke out downstairs, originally in the family room.

Sam was reading seed catalogs, which I took as a mark of high optimism on his part, but that's what he was doing—reading the old Jackson and Perkins and making notes on an order blank, if you can believe that for an early November night. He was on the other side of the kitchen divider in the little sitting room there in his recliner, so I had been able to get a shot of what he was doing from time to time over his shoulder. Sometimes, if you don't watch him, Sam-in-the-cold gets carried away and orders more seed than the USDA could use in its whole system of test gardens, so I was watching in self-defense as well as out of curiosity about what he was yearning for this year.

The rumbling was at first only louder-than-usual voices, both male. Then the music got turned up, as if in an attempt on one boy's part to drown out another boy's comment. A door—probably the family room one, from the sound of it—banged, and banged hard. The voices rose, one plainly outside the family room and one muffled from inside it. There was a scuffle involving the door.

In a house full of boys, I had long since quit trying to defend our doors, so all I did was speak firmly down the stairwell with "Boys!" and go back to waxing the stove top. The noise subsided just long enough for me to work around one of the rear eyes. Then bang went a bedroom door and up went the music.

Rebecca came down to the kitchen from her room, a five-foot bundle of righteous indignation in a too-small bathrobe. "Mother! Make them quit that! That music is coming right up into my room and I can't do a thing till it stops!"

"Boys, cut down the music."

"Yes'm," a voice chuckled . . . sounded more like John than Sam junior, but I couldn't be sure. One thing was certain, though. They weren't fighting, they were scuffling. I could hear the other voice giggle in a deep masculine tone of impudence.

The music went down, but the minute it did the noises it had been designed to cover came up to the kitchen. The brass tongs and poker on the hearth fell or got knocked over and made an awful clank, even up in the kitchen. A chair must have tipped or been shoved because a lower wall resounded, also audible in the kitchen.

"Mother!" said Rebecca, once more in the kitchen door and twice as righteous as before.

"They're not hurting anything, Bec. They're just scuffling."

"I can't do my math!"

Another door slammed.

"And I can't do my catalog!" roared the voice in the recliner. Becca could taste victory and grinned. I waited, polishing rag in mid-careen. Sam stepped to the head of the stairwell and called down, "Boys!"

69

A deep and much less chuckly voice hesitated and then offered halfheartedly, "Yes, sir."

"Come here."

The door to the family room opened and two essentially grown male children, both well over six feet, stood in the light of the lower hall looking up at the paternal wrath. "Yes, sir," said the braver one.

"You both stop that right now and behave!" (I love firmness in a man!) "Because," the father figure went on very sharply, "if you don't, your mother will end up putting you into another book and then think where you'll be!" The power figure in my life turned on its heels, patted my rear as it passed the stove, and returned to its recliner and its catalog.

Peace reigned supreme except I heard, way below me and in normal conversational tones, one voice say to the other, "He's probably right too, ya know." And there was no more unseemly behavior for the rest of that night or even the rest of that week.

It was, in fact, the total effectiveness of Sam's quasi-threat that worried me. "Do you," I asked Becca one afternoon the next week, "do you mind my writing about you and your brothers?"

"No, not particularly. I can't remember when you didn't."

Good point. I guess she really can't, though I had not thought about it before I asked my question.

"But why do you do it?" she interrupted my thoughts. "I mean, why not invent people like other writers?"

"Other writers really don't, you know. They talk about the people and places they've known too. They just don't tell you their real names."

"So, why don't you do that? Call me Elizabeth or Priscilla and make me up from little bits of me and Mary and Laura and Nora and maybe even you."

"Because I don't want to, Sweetheart. Because you're so exactly you that I don't want to mess that up by changing you around."

"If I'm so right, you sure waste a lot of time fussing about half the stuff I do."

70 And she was gone before I could tell her that I had never

said she was so right the way she was, just that she was so Rebecca the way she was . . . and that that was what I loved and what I keep trying to catch in words.

Because she was only twelve last November, it didn't seem likely that she would have understood what I was trying to tell her even if she had stayed to give me a chance, but I tried on the bear in the recliner one night.

"I agree with Rebecca," he said when I had finished. "It'd be a lot less scary for them if you'd quit preserving what they are and go to writing what they think they should be."

"But the way they are is what I love," I wailed. "If they can't accept that, they'll never let go enough to be all they really are."

"I know that and you know that," he responded. "It's just that none of us ever accepts it about himself.". . . which comment gave me a whole new insight into why Calvary had to happen. It also, I must confess, gave me no small portion of Becca's scaredness all of a sudden.

8

Time Holds Me Green and Dying

*W*hen we first moved to the Lucy Goosey Farm, I spent a lot of my time outdoors—not doing chores, everyone does that in the country—but just sitting. At the time of our move, I was, with the exception of my columns and my book reviews, still writing almost entirely in poetry.

One of the best things—perhaps the single most agreeable thing, in fact—about writing poetry is that somehow it gives one license to just sit. While most folks tend to deprecate poetry and poets, they are still, nonetheless, perfectly willing to allow us to be a bit strange and a bit inactive. It was, then, my status as poet rather than my role as farmer's wife and country mother which I exercised a lot that first year or two when I was doing my sitting.

My sitting spots were almost always in the back hammock or in the front yard. From the hammock one gets a very particularized view of things. It is one of those fishnet types of hammocks that we have had now for years. When it was new, it was dead white and springy. In its old age it has taken on a yellowish tinge and lost its elastic soul, rather like its owners, but its view is still unimpeachable.

Sam hung the hammock—and the children each spring since have re-hung it—between two of the huge pine trees that line the fence separating our backyard from our upper pasture. Lying in the hammock, one therefore looks straight up into a forest scene that would do honor to a Tolkien story. It's hard sometimes, lying there in August with the sweat of West Tennessee summertime dripping off your every limb, to remember, despite the heat, that you are not indeed in a Germanic wonderland.

Over the years of our resting there, the pines have provided a kind of microcosm of arboreal life for us to watch as we recline. Their latest gift to us came three years ago when, for the first time, a family of crows dared to enter our turf and set up housekeeping.

Much to my delight and the children's fascination, they finally decided to nest in the very uppermost reaches of one of the pine trees. From the hammock, their nest looks like a massive tree house built of limbs and branches. The birds' ability to fashion such a thing is an ongoing amazement to whoever is lying in the hammock at the moment.

But the hammock's view, as I said, is far too particularized to allow the mind to wander aimlessly. That happens better in the front yard where there are fewer specifics to attach to.

My front yard sitting, in those early days, was almost always done on the ground. I despise ants and other things that go crawling in the sunlight, so it is a mark of my absorption that I kept putting my body down on their terrain, but I did.

I don't remember much about those hours of daydreaming and listening the first couple of summers. The day I do remember, however, was in mid-October of our second year when the weather had just begun to turn a bit and the heat had relented. It was a brooding kind of day, the kind I love most for its promise of change and its whisper of power.

At the upper end of the front yard and walled in on three sides where the orchard fence joins to the backyard fence which in turn joins to the east corner of the house itself, there is a little peninsula of yard which, because it is essentially isolated, has almost nothing growing in it except grass, the ivy that keeps creeping off the house to threaten it, and a silver maple tree. The maple itself is not very large . . . never will be, I suspect, because it is caught between orchard, house, and pines.

73

I had, for some reason, not paid any more attention to the maple and its area than had the rest of the family during our early days on the farm. Even in my sitting, I had never sat there. But on this October day, because the wind was picking up and the air had turned a bit nippy, I wandered into the side yard where the maple was and sat down on its roots with its trunk as a backrest.

Before me, from that angle, lay the whole of the front acre that we call a yard and the grass-cutting boys call a plagued nuisance. Beyond it was the vine-covered fence, below which, though I couldn't see it, runs the county highway on which we face. Rising above our fence, where I could see them, were the rolling pastures of Bill Reed's land. Above the far rise of his pasture I could see the clouds banking in from the south and, caught in them, the dark smoke from the chemical plants that lie between us and the city.

Big black ants, unimpressed by the first chill of winter, began to crawl off the tree and on to me and I sat killing them as they came, until they finally got the message or ran out of troops. As I sat on, unmolested and therefore much easier, the sky began to darken and the light to silver. There would be a storm sometime before nightfall, one coming upriver from the Gulf. It would be full of heat until it hit our cool air and then it would be full of fury over being thwarted. But the clouds were coming slowly, driven by a halfhearted wind that, by dragging its feet, let me watch its parade of intentions.

There was no sound anywhere except the passing of the wind through the silver maple tree. I knew, and every bird and tree and cow on that place knew, that when the clouds finally came close enough for our cool to ingest them, the fall rains would begin. Summer would be over. Summer would be over, in fact, sometime within the next two to three hours.

Sitting on the roots of the stunted maple with my back pushed hard into its bark, I was as quiet as the world, watching the clouds shift slightly to the east, roil forward, then be sucked back westward by the river's greater warmth. But regardless of how they hesitated, diverted, and re-aligned, they were coming steadily onward. I felt like Dylan Thomas at Fern Hill. Time held me green and dying that almost-three-hours that it took for the drops to begin.

Big, heavy drops wrung from unwilling clouds and sent large enough to drown the last of summer. I let the drops turn to rain on my skin and sat on until the young maple's roots were islands in the puddles everywhere around us. But still I sat on.

In my head, inside my self where I was non-corporeal and dry, there was a whole, vast film library of Lucy Gooseys I was enjoying. Some of them were sunlit and warm; some were buried in last winter's deepest snow and filled with the sounds of our first Christmas; some were at harvesttime when we had all been so tired we couldn't even bathe before we fell into bed; some were spring when the orchard was in full bloom and the asparagus crowns were ripe and the raspberries were still green in the patch.

Sitting there, watching my memory-movies while autumn rained around me, I knew that if Time holds us green and dying, that's all right with me. I have loved Time as much as it has loved me, and it's always good when one can do one's dying in the arms of a lover.

9

A-Forging
We Will Go

Sam junior has taken up blacksmithing. Looking back, none of us is quite sure, including Sam junior, about when the thing began to overtake him.

When he was younger, the farrier would always come early on Sunday mornings, so early in fact that I would see the smoke coming across the orchard from the barn before I could even start the coffee. Since we never knew the farrier's schedule, other than that he would come on a Sunday, it was always like a lovely little surprise to smell his fire and see his smoke through the gray half-dawn.

Every time he came, I would call Sam junior to come and see; and every time he would, hanging on to the sill of the sitting room window, trying to see through the trees but managing to see only smoke and blurred shapes moving.

"Why don't you go out there?" I asked more Sundays than a few. But he would always shake his head and just watch, with obvious longing, a scene he could not possibly have been really seeing at such a distance. There was, though, something about the intensity—almost the yearning—of his watching even then that must have caught my attention and caused me to always call him the moment I saw the farrier's smoke.

When he was eleven and just beginning to have money of

his own earning, he spent almost twelve dollars to buy from a mail-order catalog a book on forging and forges. It was an odd choice for a boy, but I dutifully took his cash and wrote the catalog people a check to accompany his order. In due time his book came. I think it must have been something of a disappointment for him, because I never heard much about it after that excited afternoon when it finally came in the mail and he retreated for the rest of the day down to his room to read.

Shortly after the book, however, and despite his reticence with the farrier, he began to show an active interest in watching smithies. The fall he was twelve, we stood as a family for almost an hour in the broiling heat of September so he could watch a smith perform his wonders at the county fair. When I finally gave out and insisted that we go for ice cream, he persuaded his father to stay with him instead, "for just a little longer."

When we got back to them half an hour later, they were both inside the roped-off area with the blacksmith himself. He was showing Sam junior how one tests an anvil by its ring before buying it. While I watched, the boy took the hammer and, with the older man's guidance, rang the iron to hear that it was true.

As we were finally leaving, I said to Sam senior, "Does this mean we're getting an anvil next?"

"Who knows?" he shrugged. "A kid could be interested in worse things"—which I had to admit was true. I just wasn't sure about more bizarre things.

But the anvil would have to wait a while. It was way beyond the reach of his capital, even if he had been at the beginning of grass-cutting time, rather than at its ending. He entertained himself in the meanwhile by hanging around the smithy tents at re-enactments.

Now folks who have never seen a re-enactment have missed one of our culture's most contradictory sports. Technically, the name is now "Living History" because even the term "re-enactment" proved too contradictory. Regardless of the name one uses, however, the event still involves the re-enacting of a famous battle from some war or other. In our

77

part of the country, that means from the War Between the States specifically.

Living History also involves tenting out for a whole weekend (battles are always re-fought on Sunday afternoon, regardless of the day and hour of the original) with lots of food and drink and tale-telling.

It is a habit we married into, so to speak. Sam and I grew up in East Tennessee, which never even seceded from the Union in the first place and which has voted Republican, both literally and figuratively, in all its daily customs ever since. The Civil War and even the South as a complex of ideas were totally alien to Sam's heritage, and at least geographically distanced from mine, as a child.

My parents were West Tennesseans by birth and my father's father had gone down at Shiloh, so there was a strong family tradition of virulent pride in the 158th Senior Infantry of the Army of Tennessee. But none of my East Tennessee playmates, Yankees to the nines, all of them, ever did anything to reinforce my Rebel heritage, so I grew up thinking of my background as somewhat idiosyncratic even if treasured. Which is why I say we came to the matter of Civil War re-enactments by marriage—actually Nora's marriage.

Born and reared in West Tennessee in the veritable heartland of some of the South's major battle sites, Nora inhaled with her first cry the air of Southern traditions. My previously idiosyncratic background with its concomitant Confederate captain of a grandfather readily became a ticket into her natal society. In less than two decades it became her ticket into that of her new husband's.

Devereaux was a serious student of history and of Confederate history in particular. He is now, in fact, probably the authority on Confederate law. But originally he was just a kid, not that much older than Sam junior is now, who liked to go camping and fight battles and who, in time, took his new bride with him, and in time then her brothers and eventually her sisters, and then her parents, and now his own son.

So on any given summer weekend some re-enactment or other is likely to have stripped our house bare of kids and not infrequently of parents as well, especially if the one in question is close and doesn't involve tenting for Mama. History is one thing, but chiggers are ridiculous, in my opinion.

So off they—we—go to a battle site where our boys will stand as Southern men stood a hundred and twenty-five years ago, sweating in gray wool and brandishing polished bayonets. They will fire period pieces or facsimiles of their own careful making. The limited amount of shot that is actually fired will, for our part at least and for most, be shot that they have themselves poured and molded. The black powder will be in packets they have themselves wrapped. The cannon will be those which have survived the century and a quarter by benefit of loving care and careful maintenance; and the flags will have been made with equal reverence on dozens of sewing machines, including ours, in the dark days of winter when fighting was not, and still is not, feasible.

The guns and the cannon will be aimed at blue-clad lines of men and boys who have traveled south from as far away as Michigan and Iowa to stand along the earthworks and to hold the lines that are their heritage. They too will fire cannon of a century's vintage and shoot rifles they have constructed or passed, father to son, for decades.

In the evenings, the boys in blue will drink many a beer with the boys in gray, but at sunup on Sunday conviviality stops and the singing from each camp rises patriotic and pure right up till the moment when the battle master fires the gun that begins the games. Once more the battle is fought in dead earnest and occasionally even with minor injury.

Each camp has the requisite hospital wagon and surgeon on duty. Generally speaking, he is a physician in real life as well as in history, but his bag will contain only those drugs and supplies which would have been—or perhaps were—available in the last half of nineteenth-century medicine. And each camp will also have the attendant ancillary personnel the original camps would have had.

The sutler's tent is always a favorite with the children, as well as the quartermaster's. But for Sam junior the smithy four years ago became, and has remained, the tent of fascination. For one whole summer he spent his re-enactments in the smithy, watching and asking. He still showed almost no interest in seeing the cavalry's horses shod, but he was seduced by the grappling hooks and the cooking spits and the plow points.

That fall, when the re-enactments were done for another year and school had recommenced, he asked permission to try his hand at using the outdoor grill as a forge. "It'll never work," said Sam, at a level of non-conviction that made me ask him later if he had meant it. "Well," he said, "let's say that if the kid can make it work, he cares more about forging than I ever would."

But the kid made it work. Imperfectly, to say the least. And he had to work at it for almost three weeks before he learned to build a fire that was intense enough to turn an old poker red and glowing, but he did it.

One chilly afternoon as we were watching through the kitchen window while the boy worked on the patio beyond us, Sam senior abruptly said to nobody in particular, "OK, that does it! He deserves help."

The next afternoon an old pull motor came home from the office. The two of them rigged a bellows out of it by connecting the motor to a length of pipe and then suspending the pipe from the patio lamppost. With the ability to blow on his fire and to control more perfectly the direction of that blowing, things picked up.

Papaw, Sam's father, had been a man of many talents and had had the tools to exercise all of them. The tools, almost icons since his death, had all stayed carefully locked and unused in our garage. Now Sam opened the chest and gave the boy his grandfather's iron mallet. It was one of the more significant moments of our lives and one I have trouble seeing clearly without a rush of emotion.

The boy was fully aware of what he had been given and he took the gift for what it was; he took it with reverence. Grasping it in his hand, he swung it a time or two to get its weight before he went out and began to build his fire. That late October evening he made his first piece, a simple hook that he thought was the most handsome thing he had ever seen and so did we.

That Christmas, Devereaux and Nora gave him a leather apron that Devereaux had cut in the authentic way from a tanned hide and strung with authentic leather laces. Devereaux the Third gave him the leather soap and creme with which to care for the apron for a lifetime. We gave him fireproof gloves. The following summer he got his anvil.

For the past two summers he has been building a forge across the fencerow in the upper pasture. He works at it as time and his cash flow will allow him to acquire what he needs. Meanwhile, until he is able to complete its construction, his forge is still the patio barbecue pit. Because chores in the summer and school activities in the spring and fall keep him occupied until late afternoon, he has taken to working nights until well after dark. We will see him there sometimes long after the dishes are done and I have closed the kitchen for another night.

He will be standing in front of his fire—six feet tall and filling out the apron that looked so enormously disproportioned three years ago. It is supple now from hours of creaming and soaping. It is also discolored in that good way of leather which has known the uses it was tanned for.

The anvil sits on the patio wall beside him and the homemade bellows still directs its oxygen through garden hose and old conduit, but the results are much more sophisticated now. The family as well as some company compatriots have come to expect his forge to provide utensils and tools in much the same way that any other smithy would. The hammer rings and the sparks fly and the glow of the fire rises and falls with the switch on the old pull motor as he works, his arms and hands illuminated by the fire in front of him.

I told Sam senior one night, as the boy was shutting down for the evening, that our son looked like Vulcan forging in the dark out there.

"Vulcan on the patio?" he laughed. "That's carrying anthropomorphism at bit too far."

"How about theomorphism?" countered Nora, who, with the two Devereauxs, was home for a visit and watching with us.

81

"How's that?" said her father.

"Well, watching him," said big sister, "I find it a lot easier to believe that we were made in the image of God than to believe that we have conceived of God in our own."

Just at that moment, the back door swung open and our Vulcan stomped in, slapping his gloves together as he came.

"Hi, everybody! Whatcha watching?"

"Basic Religion 101-102," Nora answered, and we all three laughed at his confusion.

10

Runaway Son

Everyone has a "worst day of my life" story. Some folks I know even have two or three, and can invent five or six more upon demand. I'm not that good. I only have a "worst half-a-day of my life" story, and I have never told even that before now. For one thing, mine doesn't lend itself to the usual conversation at social gatherings, and for another, it has no casual ending and very little humor to it. Indeed, mine is the kind of story that seems appropriate only in a collection, like this, of private epiphanies.

We had been back living on the farm for almost a year when it happened. It was early April, that brooding time when, as Eliot says, God makes lilacs out of the dead December. Only that's in London. In West Tennessee, God has not yet got to the lilacs by April; He's still working on the peach trees and the dogwoods.

Anyway, the earth was brooding like any mother about to deliver, and it was my favorite kind of day, probably because I can empathize from so much prior experience of my own. The sky was not sunlit. That is, there was no sunshine as such, but a blanket of milky gray clouds through which the most electric and radiant of lights seemed to be seeping. The trees along the fencerow and down in the close, although they had not fully budded yet, were just green enough to catch the light and distort it into a kind of ghostly shimmer through which no breeze moved.

The older children were at school and Rebecca was back in her crib, settled in for her always long morning nap. Only Sam junior and I were up and about.

Even at not quite six, he was already my philosopher. Unlike John, who liked to roam the acres in search of whatever might present itself to him for his consideration or assimilation, young Sam liked simply to find a place and sit. Whatever came to him for assimilation was either non-corporeal or itself highly mobile.

His favorite sitting place was down at the pond; his second down in the cemetery that abutted our lower pasture; his third the magnolia tree in the front yard. The problem with the first two was that they were forbidden to him without the company of an older sibling, a restriction that somewhat compromised their function as places for effective rumination.

The cemetery was simply too far away for me to have a five-year-old go without supervision. Besides, there is a fairly treacherous bog between the pasture and the cemetery fence. As for the pond, it was a bog—a deep, deep bog—as far as I was concerned.

Certainly the cattle moved in and out of it easily. (I had ascertained its gentle slopings toward its own depths during the previous summer by watching how high in the water the cows stood as they came and went cooling themselves.) But I also saw, around its edges and down in its waters, the roots and limbs and plant life that won't restrain a cow but will drown a child.

The pond was the only horror for me on the farm, the one part of our world that had troubled my joy in being here. It had, in truth, brought me up wide awake and with a pounding heart on at least half a dozen occasions since our coming to the farm. Always the dream was the same: I saw the face of one child or another, eyes open and hair floating, staring blankly up at me through the pond's brown waters. While some Freudian could probably make something of that, all I bothered to make of it was the reality of the terror the dream caused me and the incontestable truth of the pond's danger.

Sam junior had always seemed to sense the intensity of my fear and the immutability of my rules. As a result, he had not tested them in the ten months we had been here. For my own part, I had leaned over backwards to see that some unwilling sister or brother had accompanied him to the pond at least one time out of every two or three that he asked to go. So I had relaxed somewhat in the knowledge that we had a reasonable working arrangement held up by honor and good intentions at both ends.

Even at five he showed every evidence of being a good kid . . . sloppy beyond any hope of repair, absentminded to a fault, and possessed of the family temper, but not rebellious. In fact, it was he who could always be counted on to do the kind thing, the perfect thing. The supportive gesture, the really intuitive drawing, the imaginative Mother's Day card always came from him. In return he really didn't seem to want much . . . some space, a chance to be left alone for a healthy hunk of his day, and an occasional audience for his long and detailed recitations of what he had seen and thought or almost seen and almost thought on any given day.

It was the long recitations that usually got to us. After about ten minutes of listening—even of pretending to listen—to the exact process by which he thought the hornets probably make those nests and by which he proposed the next day to attempt a similar product, I wanted to scream. His sisters usually did. His brothers simply threatened him with early death.

On this particular morning, therefore, it was not unusual that he had followed every step I made from table to sink and dishwasher, from bed to bed, from bathroom to washroom, demanding every motion or two that I "stop that!" and look at him while he showed me with his hands what he was trying to tell me about with his words . . . about how he could take all the cedar posts left over from fencing the yard and haul them to the pasture to make a house, about how he could use the fence itself for the back wall of his house, about how he could roof it with some of the tin from the barn, about how he would have to move the extra bricks behind the shed to the pasture to put down for a floor, about how he would have to put the lawn chairs in front to keep the cows from knocking it down,

85

about how . . . Finally I screamed. Not loudly—Rebecca was already asleep by then—just emphatically. The best I could remember later, I said my share of devastating things about his longevity if he didn't hush right now and either go do it or quit talking it to death.

"OK," he said with his usual cheerfulness when he is rebuffed, and out the front door he went. I do remember thinking it a mark of his fundamental good humor that he could always tell when he had pushed it too far and forgive us for our resulting explosions. But beyond that I paid him no mind. I did check once, a half hour or so later, to see if I could spot an area of denim blue in the top of the magnolia. I could and that was the end of that.

With Rebecca still soundly snoring that incredible snore two-year-olds give when they are into serious sleeping, I went out the back door with absolutely no purpose in mind than to enjoy. That kind of day only comes about twice a year around here, and any other chores I might have could wait for another, more mundane day. I sat on the back steps for a while, feeling the life around me, absorbing the energy of the luminous light. Eventually I moved to the patio wall in order not to have even the house blocking me. The sense of air all around me was comforting and I thought, as I sat there, that young Sam might just have come by some of his strange ways honestly.

Wouldn't it be nice to take him down to the pond for a little while, sort of as a forgiveness gesture for having cut his pasture house off so shortly? I checked my watch. Becca was good for another forty-five minutes at least.

I went around to the magnolia tree. No Sam junior. I couldn't believe it! I looked again. Sure enough, the top of the tree was empty. I called. No answer.

"He's begun his house," I thought. I went to the stack of leftover railings. No little boy and no evidence that one had even been there.

"His room," I thought, going back in the house. He wasn't there either . . . but his fishing hat was gone!

There was no way he could have made it to the pond without my seeing him from the patio wall . . . unless he'd slipped deliberately out his door, around the house, through the orchard to the barn, and then down below the hillock. "Why in the world would he do that?" I asked myself. "To get there," I answered myself. "To get there without being stopped."

I could hear in my head all the things I had said to him less than an hour earlier, how I had sent him off to his own devices and told him—told him both sharply and sincerely—to entertain himself.

I made it to the pond without even stopping for my boots, slipping, sliding, and stumbling as I went. No Sam junior. I raced around the whole perimeter, damning the murkiness of the water and the eeriness of the light. I could see nothing—absolutely nothing. The waters were impenetrable. No. He couldn't be. He wouldn't have, I told my pounding heart. I raced back up, calling, yelling, screaming as I went.

Gasping for air with which to call and still to climb, I made it back to the house. No little boy anywhere and no response to my calls.

The cemetery. Surely he was at the cemetery. But no way to get there and leave Becca. No way to go through the bog with Becca. I raced to the phone to call the only neighbors we have. Thank God! The line was busy! Someone was home!

As it turned out, only Mr. Williams was home, but it didn't take two seconds to look at me and know we were in trouble. He beat me by several minutes back to our side of the fence line and was halfway to the cemetery before I got back to the house. By the time I had checked Becca once again and got back outside, he was coming back from the cemetery. No Sam junior.

Then he said the thing we were both thinking. "Did you check down in the pond?"

"Yes." I could feel the tears of panic rising up.

"With a pole?"

"Oh, God," I cried, my night visions swimming in front of me. "No."

"Stay with the baby and keep hollering for him. If I don't find him, we'll have to call the sheriff." Then he added, "You'd

87

best go call your husband." And he was gone, but in his bluntness he had put an end to all my agitation.

It had been almost an hour since I had last seen the spot of blue denim in the magnolia top, and well over an hour and a half since I had told my son to go away and leave me alone. A farm has lots of places to hide, but ours has none outside the sound of adult voices unless a little boy can't answer or won't. It was that simple. Whatever had happened, had already happened. It could no longer be feared; it was.

I went in and called Sam, telling him what had happened, telling him he had better come, telling him even that I thought there was a good chance Sam junior had run away because I had refused to listen to him. "I'm coming," was all Sam said and the line went dead.

Bill was right. I needed to go back to hollering, to doing something.

I went out the back door and turned my head to begin projecting my voice when I saw the streak of blue running a broken field through the pine trees along the fencerow, making for the front of the house. As he broke out of the protection of the trees and into the open space, I saw him clearly, the fishing hat still on his head and the jigs bouncing brightly as he ran. "Sam! Sam!" I half-screamed, half-commanded.

He stopped in mid-leap, saw me and sank into dejected submission. He had made no more than two steps toward me before I had made it all the way to him and was holding him tighter than any child has ever been held before. "Baby, baby, baby," was all I could say and then the tears came. Convulsive, racking tears that only stopped when I realized that I was terrifying him.

When I finally managed to get hold of myself and look up, there stood Bill Williams watching us, a dripping pitchfork still in his hand.

"I found him," I said feebly.

"I see," he said and waited for me to finish feeling along every inch of the little body I was holding, as if to assure myself through my hands that he was indeed mine again and all right.

When I was done and had sat the child back down, Bill said

quietly, "Come here, son," and held out his hand. The boy went slowly, almost reluctantly, taking the proffered adult hand. The two of them went out of earshot and sat down together on the patio wall where, a lifetime ago, I had myself so peacefully sat. What they said to each other we never exactly knew, but the child told us part of it.

After Bill had gone home, covered in our thanks, and after Rebecca was settled down with the afternoon edition of "Sesame Street," Sam senior, Sam junior, and I faced each other over what was left of our lunches. "Why?" his father asked him.

"I don't know," he shrugged.

"Yes, you do know," Sam senior said.

He loves a story too well not to eventually give in, and besides, one of his stories had our total attention for the first time in days. "Because," he began, in that maddening way of his. "Because . . . well, because at first I didn't mean to. . . ." Then it began to pour out of him. "I mean I guess I didn't hear Mama at first, and then she was really mad when I did hear her. And I was scared to come. I was only in the garage anyway, and so when she came in the house, I went back to the magnolia."

"That was it?" I interrupted him without thinking. He had been so intent on his own story that my question seemed to disconcert him.

"No, m'am." He shook his head as if remembering and then tried again. "When you started looking in the yard, I came back this way and hid in the well house," he said finally.

"That's where you were?" his father asked.

"Yes, sir. Until Mama went to the pond. Then I went back to the garage until she went to get Mr. Williams. When she did that, I went to the shed."

I was stunned. He had watched every move I had made, countering each with a move of his own like two players in some kind of elaborate chess game. "Why didn't you just answer me?"

"Because," he said. "Like I told you. It was just fun at first 89 and then I got scared to come home." Suddenly the tears welled up in his own eyes. "I was so afraid."

"Afraid?" I said. It had never occurred to me that there was any fear except parental involved here. "Afraid? What in the world were you afraid of?"

"I was so afraid you wouldn't find me and I would have to stay outside all night!" And he began to weep great, deep, agonizing sobs of relief.

"You knew Mama would find you," Sam soothed.

"No I didn't," he muffled his voice into Sam's neck as his father held and rocked him.

"But all you had to do was answer me," I protested.

The little strawberry blonde head shook back and forth against the protecting chest a time or two before our son turned just enough to say, "I couldn't. You would've killed me if I'd answered before you got good and worried."

He was right of course. One of us was going to have to bear the pain of our reconciliation and better me than him, at least from his point of view—probably even from mine, I finally decided, as I watched him snuffling up the last of his tears.

"What did Mr. Williams say to you?" Sam asked.

"He said what I did wasn't funny, 'specially since I could really have been hurt or dead. He said you both love me an awful lot."

"Is that all he said to you?"

"Well," he cut his eyes up at Sam through long, wet lashes and grinned. "He also said he would personally beat my butt if I ever did it again."

"Good for Mr. Williams." Sam was struggling to suppress an inappropriate grin of amusement and release. I was having the same problem at my end of the lunch table.

"Yes, sir. He seemed mighty sincere about it."

"I suspect he was," Sam managed to say without loss of sobriety.

"Yes, sir"—and he went to fall asleep in front of Big Bird and the Cookie Monster.

But that night, as one by one the others went to their rooms and to their beds, I delayed my own going. Even after Sam had finally gone on up without me, I could not force myself toward rest. My gratitude for a child in every bed this night was cut through by my dread of what might lie ahead.

The dream of the child in the pond, while it had frequently disturbed me, had never been intimate enough to make me fear seeing it again. But that was no longer true. Now I understood what the dream was about. It was about guilt and absolute helplessness; and I could not commit myself to either of them again, at least not so soon. So I put off going to sleep until finally sleep would wait for me no longer. I drifted off in the easy chair where I was reading.

The next morning I awoke stiff but refreshed . . . and vaguely surprised. I rummaged through my memory for what it was that was surprising me and recalled slowly that the dream had not come; or, if it had, that it had not awakened me, which is the same thing.

It really didn't matter much on that sunny morning in my easy chair whether or not the dream of the water-killed child was gone for good; it mattered a great deal that I had lived one night (and all the nights since, in fact) on the other side of it. It mattered, and still does, that that day on the patio when Bill Williams, like some avenging angel in overalls, took a pitchfork to fish for my child, he pushed me beyond fear. He pushed me where women go so many times in our lives: into knowing that whatever is, is and that it must be accepted . . . that even the anguish it contains must be accepted.

But for me, as for my runaway on that April day, coming in where the punishing imagination isn't needed and chastising process is, is sometimes more terrifying than being left out all night with our dreams. Ironically enough, of course, it is Mr. Eliot of the December-bred lilacs—a poet, in other words, and not a priest—who talks a lot about that kind of moving in from nightmares into faith. He calls it death by water.

In the days before Bill Williams and his pitchfork, I had always thought "death by water" was just a metaphor for Christian baptism. I was wrong, of course. Baptism is a metaphor for the passage. The Christian part is learning to call the other side "Father" and understand that as a title it too has been earned with agony.

91

——— 11 ———

Don't Tread on Me

*I*n our backyard, just to the yard side of the smokehouse and almost squarely in the middle of Rebecca's spice beds, we have a flagpole, a fact that interests me more and more the longer I live with the flagpole. John put it there when he was fourteen.

We are probably the only farm in our village that has a flagpole, certainly that has one two acres from the road where only we and our more intimate visitors can enjoy it. I mentioned this peculiarity to John once. His answer was, "Mom, for goodness' sakes! I wasn't making a statement, just a flagpole!"—as clear and surgical a response, I thought, as any I have ever received from a child. It had never occurred to me that he was making anything other than a flagpole. I am of the wrong generation to have considered statements. So I hushed.

John didn't ask me about the flagpole in the first place, of course. I just assumed that he had asked his father, who, it turns out, thought that he had asked me. The result was, as it so often is with children, that he asked no one and went on, unsanctioned but unhindered, with what he was about.

Looking out a window to find some child digging a hole is so unremarkable on a farm as to almost never be remarked. I just never even recorded the fact then, on that first afternoon, that

John was digging in the spice bed. Later I remembered that I had stood at the bathroom window and wondered what in the world he was doing that near the new basil, but that was as far as I had gone with it.

I do remember watching as he and his brother, who was not quite twelve at the time, came hauling the pole into the backyard from the barn. It was, and is, a sizable piece of two-inch pipe that Sam had bought a couple of years before when he had been planning to wire the barn loft and then had later changed his mind. We, of course, had forgotten the thing was even out there, but boys rarely forget things like thirty feet of uncut pipe. So they came bearing their burden (John was bearing and Sam junior was barely bearing), but it still didn't dawn on me to ask what they were doing.

When they actually got two sacks of cement mix from the barn, I truly don't know because I didn't see that happen. The point is that at some time they did. The next thing I saw—and it was the first time I actively recorded what I was seeing (the first time, in other words, that I remember saying to myself, "I wonder if his father knows what he is doing?")—was the morning after the pole had come in from the barn and two days after the digging had begun. I looked out of the kitchen window and saw John with Sam's sawhorses beside him and the wheelbarrow beyond him.

After that, I checked from time to time as my household routine would take me by a window. I saw him measure and saw some used two-by-four ends into equal lengths, which he then hammered into a frame and which, as I dallied over the fresh spinach I was trying to wash, he set above the hole in the spice bed and proceeded to stomp firmly in place.

Actually it was precisely at the moment when I saw him heave a bag of cement mix and pour half of it into the wheelbarrow that I began to wonder if his father knew what he was doing. Without any hesitation, however, and with all the sureness of the authorized, he rolled the wheelbarrow over to the sand pile behind the shed, where, out of my view, I assumed he was adding sand and pea gravel to it. Sure enough, in a few minutes he came back into view with the wheelbarrow and went with it to the well house, where he

93

began to water and mix his concoction with as much apparent confidence as his father would have employed in the same chore.

It took three loads of concrete before he was satisfied that the hole and the frame were sufficiently full. Then he got his brother again (I was blatantly watching out the kitchen window by now, and Rebecca had taken a seat on the patio wall in order to get a better view), and the two of them picked up the pole and laid it straight out perpendicular from the smokehouse wall. John, being the taller, then changed places with Sam junior and went to the farther end of the pole.

There was obviously some difficulty about the next step because I could hear angry words passing between the two of them . . . something about Sam junior's being stupid and John's being a bully . . . but that's like digging on farms, so usual as to be unremarkable. After a few exchanges they apparently worked out their chain of command and went back to struggling with the pole.

This time John raised his end only after Sam junior had lifted and positioned his end firmly over the concrete-filled hole. With rather impressive skill, the two of them guided the pipe into the concrete slowly as John walked it higher and higher . . . but not high enough. They had to give up and reconsider, laying the pipe back on the grass and troweling the concrete off of it and back into the hole.

A less impassioned discussion followed, which I could not hear, but which plainly involved John's diplomatic and political skills. He must have succeeded because in a few minutes I saw him come out of the shed with Sam's heaviest and longest rope. Once more under John's direction, they picked up the conduit and aligned it with the hole. This time, when John had walked the thing as high as he could, Sam junior looped the rope above John's hands toward the upper end of the pole and secured it.

"Good boys," I thought proudly as he slung the rope over John's extended arms and carried the other end of it around to the front of the smokehouse and threw it up on the roof. As I watched, he climbed up the far wall of the low building, walked across its flat roof, and retrieved the rope. John meanwhile was begging him to hurry. Even in the kitchen, that much was plainly audible.

I was torn between a strong urge to go relieve my son and a strong instinct that said to leave him alone. Before I could decide between the two, Sam junior had looped his end of the rope around the chimney and lashed it there. John let go and Sam junior climbed down. They crossed paths as John headed up and Sam junior headed toward the spice bed.

John unlashed the rope and, using the chimney as a pulley (had his father really agreed to this?), he began to pull the pole upright while Sam junior continued to hold its other end firmly on target in the concrete. It took the two of them at least fifteen minutes, but they got it done. That was the moment when it dawned on me what I had been so docilely watching off and on for two and a half days.

I didn't say anything, but feeling guilty and more than a little anxious, I went back to my work. In a few minutes Becca came in and began to help me with the apples I was peeling. Then Sam junior came in hot and hungry for lunch. "Did you put up the tools?"

"John's washing up the wheelbarrow now," he said.

"What are you doing out there?"

"Making John a flagpole."

It was the only possible answer and the one I had dreaded. "How is he going to hang a flag on it?" My words were heavy in my own mouth, as a mother's so often are, and bitter with the memory of some of my own failed projects.

"Oh, no," he said and was back out the door without even drying his hands off.

We didn't eat lunch that day, or at least not as a family. Becca and I had a snack as we finished the apples, but neither boy came in until almost suppertime except for supplies and Cokes.

To tell the truth, I had no idea how one made a flagpole out of a length of conduit, and I still don't know exactly how John did out of ours, although he explained it to us in great detail, complete with drawings, that night after supper. (Whatever he did is still working four years later, so it must have been effective.)

The best I can tell, he and Sam junior gerry-rigged a cap to the pole by wrapping wire around and around it. Some of the wire they then plaited into a homemade loop. It was through this loop that they ran, again without parental foreknowledge, an eighty-foot hunk of my new clothesline—which had only been a hundred feet in the first place. (Have you any idea how difficult it is to find a use for twenty leftover feet of new clothesline?)

The only reason I did not protest the clothesline, once I had discovered it, was that I had indeed watched from the window while the pole, erected at such cost, had had to be lowered carefully back to the ground and the concrete once more troweled off its base and back into the hole before the upper end could be wired and strung. Because I had also watched as the pole, about four o'clock that afternoon, was reset with just as much effort and shouting as had been required the first time. Because I saw the hands that came in to be washed for supper. They were red from working in the cement certainly and pricked in numerous places by the bits of wire that had broken off in them. More to the point, they had left pink spots on my tea towel after John had dried his.

We ate supper and we talked over the contrivance that had turned the pipe into a pole and, later that night after bedtime, two of us discovered that neither of us had known what was going on in the first place.

A week or so later, when the cement had firmly set, John went back up the smokehouse wall and released the rope that had held the pole in place. Back on the ground, he thwacked the pole a time or two, taking obvious pleasure in its answering bong and in its controlled swaying. Sam had brought home two two-way swivel hooks one evening, and John took them now and secured them to my erstwhile clothesline. Then he truly surprised me.

He went to his room, got something out of his bottom drawer, and went back outside. In a matter of five minutes or so, we had the Bonnie Blue Flag of Texas flying in our backyard. I had previously had no idea that we cared a whit about Texas, much less that we owned a copy of her Bonnie Blue. Apparently that was because we hadn't always. John had found this one at a school rummage sale and had bought it with his own money because he thought it handsome.

That Christmas Sam and I gave him a Gaston flag, all triumphantly yellow, fiercely snaky, and full of our world-view. But John said that its "Don't Tread on Me" was definitely too much of a message (I had bought the thing before asking my question), and he has flown it little.

Texas' Bonnie Blue has been joined, therefore, by flags more to his own liking. The Stars and Bars flies rather frequently, as does the flag of the Confederate States of America, a gift from Nora and Devereaux. There is also a growing collection of truly brilliant wind socks that get run up on jolly occasions and a rather faded battle flag or two on ones that aren't. Overall, the pole has added a certain festive, if nonpolitical, flair to things.

The only message, so far as I know, that our pole has ever been asked to convey was one night when the Bishop was coming for supper and, lacking a flag of the Church, John innocently ran the Union Jack up as our nearest available substitute. Since, unknown to John, things weren't going too well with Canterbury at that time, I don't think the Bishop was amused, but his father and I were, which is always enough for most youngsters, including ours.

The flagpole, much as we have enjoyed it, was only the first of John's projects. Shortly after he hung his first flag, he began to run a retaining wall around the flower beds on either side of the back steps. It was a job that badly needed doing, and I was truly grateful for his doing it. The beds there were yard level and spilled their dirt, weeds, and debris constantly onto the patio. Even Becca was beginning to complain that she could never get the thing swept clean because of those darned beds. By August of that fourteenth summer, and with the Stars and Stripes in full sway above him, John had hauled brick and mixed concrete and raised a wall ten inches high around the beds. He had also hauled dirt and raised the beds to accommodate the height of the wall.

Then, as a kind of an aside, he had dug and re-secured the loose handrail that goes from the back door down the steps and into the flower bed below. The thing had become so wobbly that it was almost dangerous; yet it was still too much in place for Sam senior to stop and fix it. Consequently, I, like Rebecca, complained constantly—at a low-grade and, I'm sure, infuriating level—about the nuisance of it. Having it securely set at last was a major relief, the kind that can come only from the solving of a minor problem. My thanks were as sincere as they were profuse.

The next summer the project was the front driveway, which got extended all the way to the edge of the backyard at its upper end (a project I again had frequently mentioned as desirable) and also broadened into a turning apron along its east side.

Last summer, when his projects were enhanced by his ability to drive into town for what he wanted, we gained a garbage area, complete with ramp and secluding wall. This summer, Mary, after work and on weekends, is getting a new sidewalk to go in front of her newly purchased first house in the city . . . which is, of course, what interests me about the flagpole in the backyard.

The more I live with the pole . . . the more I am the one who enjoys running up the day's colors, for I am, of course . . . the more I am forced to admit that John's sense of abstractions has moved completely from crayons to concrete.

I used to hang his drawings on the refrigerator door and stick his *Weekly Reader* puzzles on the cabinets. Now we seem to be collecting, as well as using, creations of his that will outlast us and probably him. I thought it to be a nostalgic and not impertinent observation the other night when, while cleaning up the supper dishes, I made it to him. His only response was, "Well, I can sure tell you one thing. There was a lot less risk in making you things to hang on the refrigerator."

"What kind of risk did you have in mind?" I asked.

"The kind I didn't have to take in the first place," he said, "and that I can't hide once I have." Which would be a lot like starting babies and writing books, come to think about it, and a very sensible position to hold, if it weren't for that dreadful parable about the poor slob who hid his one talent to avoid the risk and lost himself as a result.

"Well," I said, for lack of anything more profound to say, "better to go down trying than not to try at all . . . so long as the gods keep their sense of humor, that is."

"Oh, Mother!" Sam junior said wearily from his place in front of the sitting room TV. "They call that grace, you dope, not humor."

"Strange," I said, "I have never thought of grace as being another name for divine humor!"

But the more I have thought about it since, the more I think my third son was as correct as he was unorthodox . . . and the more I have enjoyed setting that Gaston flag to flying from the top of our non-message flagpole.

THE SIGN
OF THE EAGLE

12

City Courage
and Country Kids

*J*ohn has always had bird problems. They began, like John himself, in the days of our city life.

In those years we were, as are so many young professional families in America, confined in both our living and our playing by the restrictions of careers on the move upward. Sam was, of course, building a medical practice that would both sustain us and, probably more important, satisfy his own sense of all the years of schooling and training he had gone through. Basically a writer and a merchant in words at heart, I was comfortably diverted, or perhaps just occupied, by the related business of college teaching. I was certainly totally satisfied by the consuming business of childbearing. Whatever else we were doing during those city years, we were surely learning the spendthrift joy of having all the children we wanted.

In the early days of our marriage, when Sam was in medical school and I was teaching high school Latin to pay the bills, I had miscarried time and again, a practice that was to become a pattern for me. As a result, every baby now brought successfully into the world was a gift for us, one that lay far outside the parameters of intellectual understanding or biological process.

Every new Tickle was given by an intention and a goodness unrelated to copulation. At our house, the merely human was

103

not enough to make a child; grace and miracle had to be added to the formula. Each time it was, we carried that new infant toward the baptismal font with a penetrating sense of returning to God what God had both given and caused. The words of the service could never even begin to approximate the joy of our hearts that another child had made it safely into and through birth to join us here in this experience.

So the city years were marked by their long nights of late hospital calls and 2:00 A.M. feedings; by yards that were never large enough to grow a real garden; by birthday parties in public playgrounds and family outings in municipal parks; by a progression of pets; and, inevitably, by a limited exposure for the children to the natural order. It was this last that most troubled Sam and that was to be for him right at the center of our move back to rural living.

In the meantime, however, we tried to provide the children with as many animals and responsibilities and with as much vicarious education as we could. Sometimes, mercifully, circumstances assisted us—or perhaps I should say that sometimes the natural order simply broke dramatically through civilization's projection of itself and came storming into our backyard and the children's attention.

Each of our children can recall vividly a particular event or circumstance that brought home to him or her the meaning of process and the humility of being part of some unknowable whole. As every parent can understand, the stories that our grown children now remember and retell at family gatherings about those experiences are ones that I remember either differently or not at all. No phenomenon, in fact, so attests to the truth of many worlds in one world as does an evening around the Lucy Goosey table, after supper and during a holiday, when all the bodies that have once fed here reassemble to recall those parts of childhood which each has remembered, kept, found useful, been shaped by, saved to pass on. But regardless of the multiplicity of the memories and renditions of the others, at least young John and I both remember his epiphany or rite of passage the same way and in the same detail.

104

John is now seventeen, considerably taller than I, graceful as a panther, and better-looking than is good for him. Since we moved to the farm when he was not quite seven, he has little personal memory of what city chores and city accommodations are like. He has a considerable store of information and personal experience about rural chores and country accommodations. He is, in other words, far more familiar with his own perspiration than he is with air-conditioning; but the lesson that has served him best in his country life was city given—given, in fact, by city birds.

The year John was three and Sam junior was one was an eventful one for us. My mother, after three years of living as a widow alone in East Tennessee, had closed her affairs the year before and had made plans to move west to us at just about the same moment that Sam junior was also scheduled to join us. Because we were many in number and loud in our quantity, no one had really thought that Granny could tolerate living with us or that we could tolerate the stress of watching her try. As a result, Sam, at the same time that he was busy re-staining the baby bed and building a new wardrobe, was also busy converting the "whatchamacallit" in our backyard to housing for Granny.

The whatchamacallit had obviously been many things before it became Grandma's house. Because we had had to be near the hospitals, we had taken a house in midtown Memphis, an area that had at one time been very affluent and that, during our years of living there, was to become so again. At the time that we had bought into the neighborhood, however, much of it, including our property, was what one of my friends called "shabby genteel" or what Sam called "down at the heels and damned near gone." Whatever its problems as a piece of property, though, it had location, possibilities, and space, as well as the whatchamacallit in the backyard.

The thing had, we assumed, originally been a servants' quarters in the heyday of the neighborhood. It still had evidence of plumbing and an odor that indicated that some had once been misused there. It had a room that could be interpreted as having once been a bedroom. The rest of it had been re-walled to house a car, causing us to assume that it had

105

become a garage at one period of its life. By the time we arrived, the debris scattered through all of it suggested that it had also been a shop at some stage of things, maybe even a principal mode of making a living for somebody.

Whatever the thing was or might be had been immaterial to us at the time we had moved in and begun to try to raise a family there. Sam had simply boarded up its holes and entrances, and we ignored it . . . until Granny decided it was time for her to move in. The more we had thought about a new baby and another adult in our lives at the same time, the more she and we had thought about that awful, out-back piece of a building.

There was at that time a city ordinance that allowed homeowners to make any additions they might want to their property so long as they incorporated at least one existing wall in those additions. Given the ordinance and our problem, Sam set to work on incorporating the back wall of the whatchamacallit into a solution for our forthcoming grandmother.

By the time he had got through, he had, in typical Sam fashion, created the perfect garden apartment for Granny. No one, without before and after photos, could ever have guessed that the charming backyard efficiency with the huge front porch and the large sunny windows had ever been anything else than charming and sunny or even efficient.

Once Sam and the labor he had hired to help him had finished the house, we quickly perceived the loss of about half of whatever small bit of cultivable yard we had ever had. Once Granny moved in in May, we also quickly perceived what an attractive alternative we had created for small children and toddling babies. To get away from the maternal wrath or the day's tedium, one had only to wiggle the back door open and slip—sometimes literally—down the back steps to Granny's house and a whole different and less judgmental form of nurturing.

After a year of struggling to control our emigration problem (and with no more success than that enjoyed by the Russian government with theirs, I might add), Sam had given up and decided to face facts. The straw that had finally broken the camel's back—no offense intended—had been Sam junior.

At ten months of age Sam junior had somehow taught Vickie, our oversized and over-endowed German shepherd, to open the back door for him with her teeth. Once that bit of magic had been effected, he would then crawl onto the back stoop, turn around, diaper-end up, and back down the concrete steps to the patio beyond. Having gained that much territory, he would stand up and toddle wherever the caprices of the moment and Vickie's imagination might lead them both, which usually was the intended destination of Granny's house and a little TLC for both. On two occasions unfortunately something diverted Vickie's questionable attention from Granny to the front sidewalk, and we found both making their way streetward instead of Granny-ward. The third time did it and Sam decided to deal.

It was either put a slip bolt on the back door—a dangerous procedure in a house full of little folks who for their own safety needed to be able to evacuate a house unaided should the need ever arise—dispose of Vickie, which would have killed Sam before we ever did; or fence. Fencing, despite Robert Frost's notions to the contrary, seemed to be far and away the best solution of the three.

So during the whole spring and early summer of John's third year, Granny's second, and Sam junior's first, Daddy dug post holes, sweated, cussed, and fenced after office hours and before nightfall. By midsummer he had achieved an enclosure that wrapped from midway of our west side wall, across the width of our lot, back along our property line, and across to Granny's incorporated back wall. It then picked up again beyond her porch to complete its passage across the back of the lot and back streetward to the east corner of our house. The whole was gated in front toward the driveway, in back toward the alley behind, on the side into Vickie's new dog lot (she wasn't too happy about it, but the three cats thought it was a wonderful idea), and at the upper end into the drive of our neighbors on the east. Each of the four gates proudly bore a slip latch that no dog on earth could ever be taught to throw and that was a good foot above the reach of

107

anything under ten years of age, be it human or canine. We had achieved compound, or that was what Grandmother announced the night the last nail was driven and we christened the whole with lemonade.

All that summer, then, the toddler, the dog, and the three-year-old had been Granny's constant but peripatetic companions. Their mobility had been wonderful for all of us to behold, and the dramatic jump in their space was heady in its freedoms.

All summer the air-conditioning bill soared as the three of them moved back and forth to Granny's until I finally taught them to close the back door after themselves—more accurately, until I taught John and Vickie to close it. I never managed to teach Sam junior. I finally just gave up and took to shutting it without comment every time I found it standing ajar. In all fairness I had to admit that there is a limit to what one can expect of children. After all, the dog and the three-year-old weren't wearing diapers that had to be held on to as one pivoted bellyside down on concrete steps.

So we all approached the cool days of fall that year with a sense of completion and of satisfaction that was total—and totally reinforced by the grandmother waiting at the other end of the garden's path, but safely within the confines of its new fence. Going unchecked to Granny's was the ultimate expression of freedom.

The joy of the newly reclaimed yard and back environs was enhanced in late September by the arrival of starlings. In the past, our birds had all flown north, or at least out of sight of both us and the cats, by early fall. That year, however, for the first time starlings had come to West Tennessee in considerable numbers. The boys'—particularly John's—pleasure in their raucous presence was absolute. He was as impervious to the agitation it was causing the cats as he was to the distress in many of our surrounding neighborhoods where the birds were arriving in near-invasion proportions. He was also totally innocent of the nightly television coverage of the increasing health and safety hazards the birds were causing in the downtown and airport areas.

Our birds were to him simply an unexpected and delightful extension of summer and the joys of his new space. He shot them with his finger and took serious aim at them with both his water pistol and his plastic dart gun. He chased them on his way to Granny's porch and shooed them off the twenty-some feet of sidewalk that lay between him and the way back home when he was done. He even slipped them bits of food on occasion to try to attract them. Because he was himself an appetite on wheels, the offerings were rarely any more attractive to the starlings than they had originally been to him, however. In general, though, the birds were a welcome addition to our lives, if not to the city's.

The days grew sharper as October gave way to Halloween, and Halloween to early November. John's birds grew pitiably cold and fewer in numbers. On the naked tree limbs they were more visible than they had been in the early fall, but there were never more than four or five of them at any one time for a three-year-old to take aim at as he went to Granny's, and rarely any now to shoo on the way back. Unable yet to whistle at those that remained, John had to content himself with making up stories for us about what he and the birds had done together (or, more often, what he had done to the birds) on his adventurous traversings of the backyard.

Then it was Thanksgiving week and no longer cool, but pleasantly, reassuringly cold. Daddy built and lit the fire in the family room, and we all knew from years of experience that it would continue to burn there, tended and fed by him, until spring came again. On Wednesday morning, Granny came up the garden path to spend the day cooking with us in our bigger kitchen.

After lunch the boys began to be fretful and restless from their unaccustomed confinement. We cooked on for a while, but before four o'clock Granny was either persuaded by the sincerity of their anguish or herself worn down by the confusion. She gave in and took them to her house.

By that stage of the afternoon, the holiday pies and bread and salads were all made anyway, and Sam has always done the turkey, so off she went to her house with the entourage of the faithful trailing happily along behind her. The girls and I 109 watched out the family room window as she unlocked her door, admitted two boys, denied one mammoth dog, kicked one cat gently but concisely away, and turned on her lights.

Half an hour later, when I checked again, I could see her moving about in her kitchenette starting the green bean casserole she had said she could do as easily at her house as at ours. Through her not-so-sunny-today windows, I could also see two small heads turned up toward her television; and on her porch I saw a very happy dog contentedly working on a new rawhide bone, one that certainly hadn't come from our house.

"Oh, well, " I thought, "why be a granny if you can't act like one?" As if in agreement, Vickie saw me through the window, wagged her tail perfunctorily, and went back to gnawing. "How cheaply our loyalties are bought," I told her through the closed window, but either she just didn't have any conscience at all or she simply didn't hear me. Whatever the reason, I saw no more of my crew until suppertime, when Vickie brought them all back to me and forgot, yet again, to nuzzle the door shut after herself.

Thanksgiving, which remains to this day as my favorite holiday, was lovely, the best I remember. Unlike Christmas with its unavoidable tensions and anxious expectations, Thanksgiving has all the goodness of family and interrupted routine and a long weekend without cooking or schedules. If feasting isn't exactly my favorite exercise, certainly sitting around a table after one is, and Thanksgiving allows that in a way that Christmas never can.

So we sat long that day. While the babies fell asleep on the floor and the sofa respectively, Nora and her new boyfriend (who was Devereaux and destined to become our first son-in-law in due time, though none of us knew that then) courted, and Mary and Philip and Laura watched television. The adults—Daddy, Mama, Granny, an uncle, and two aunts—swapped family tales and countless "Now whatever happened to Hap Mason's boy, the one that was born right after Hap was killed? You remember him? His sister married that fellow from down at Ridgely?" et cetera, et cetera.

There was something remarkably reassuring about knowing that the same questions and meanderings had happened at this same table every year for twenty years and would, by the grace of God, continue to happen at it for another thirty or forty, maybe more. It was, I decided sitting there, the most complete and the most exact summation of what I was thankful for each year. It was process.

But inevitably, that year as with every other year and every other Thanksgiving, the afternoon began to settle around us. The parades were over on television, the babies began to stir, and the uncle grew sleepy. Time to go our separate ways again.

Nora excused the two of them to an early movie. Granny slipped quietly out the back door before the little ones could see and follow her, claiming weariness and a strong desire to be alone as her excuse. Sam fell asleep, as he frequently does, right where he was in the host's chair. The older children and I walked the relatives to their cars, waving good-bye in the cloudy crispness of the late November cold.

Back inside, thirteen-year-old Mary and ten-year-old Laura set about the business of helping me put away the food and all the fancies that mark high feast days at most houses. Great-grandmother's turkey platter has to be washed by hand, not in the dishwasher. The gravy ladle and the dressing spoon have to be polished free of tarnish before they are returned to the silver chest, where they will stay until Christmas gets them out again. The salt and pepper have to be put back into the kitchen shakers and the silver ones washed and left out to air-dry. The butter has to be set back on an everyday plate and the crystal one carefully washed, dried, and stored back in the china closet.

And so it went for a good hour at least. The work, never unpleasant in any event, is made lighter and happier each year by happy memories and my growing satisfaction in the girls' growing skills and appreciations. Through the silver and the antiques in our hands we were weaving the final mysteries of the day, my daughters and I, or so I thought as we were doing it.

111

By three-thirty and for the first time in their lives, my girls were saying to me, "You go on, Mama. We'll babysit and finish up with the food." They were indeed growing up, and they deserved the opportunity to prove it.

"All right," I said. But, being a mother, I had to add, as I was leaving the kitchen, one last set of instructions. "Be sure you throw all those turkey bones into the cats' dishes along with the skin and the carcass. But keep your eye on Vickie until the cats have finished eating them. I don't want her choking on any of those little bones."

"Yes'm," they said with exaggerated weariness. (They had heard the same admonition after every turkey they had ever eaten in their brief number of years.) And up I went to our bedroom and my recliner for a little luxury.

It seemed to me that I had hardly settled into the chair, much less pushed it back into full relaxation, when I heard the scream. It was so piercing and so consuming that I could not even identify at first which child it had come from. It was also totally wordless, containing no message save its own horror. As I shot out of the chair and toward the stairs, Laura Lee, white-faced and breathless, came up them. But the scream came again from below her . . . came from the kitchen or the family room. "What is it?" I demanded as we met in the middle of the hallway.

"Look!" She was beyond words as she dragged me by my sleeve back through the hall to the bedroom's back windows. There below me was a tossing and undulating sea of iridescent blackness where our yard had been. The roof of Granny's house was covered, and every tree limb hung limp and heavy with the birds. There were hundreds of them. "All I did"—she was trying to tell me through her tears and her panic—"All I did was open the back door to take the turkey out. They were there before I could get back inside." And she began to tremble violently in my arms.

From downstairs I could hear the sobbing that had followed the screams and I could also hear Sam's deep voice calming the screamer. It was John, I realized, and not Laura whose terror had brought me up so abruptly. Still holding Laura's hand and reassuring her as we went, I urged her as best I could back downstairs and to the family room, where Sam stood in front of the windows holding a still hysterical three-year-old in his arms.

The noise of the birds was everywhere, more pervasive than that of the frightened children. "They must be starving," Sam said to me as he nodded toward the window. "John apparently was looking out the window when they almost got Laura Lee." The boy cringed visibly and snuggled closer into the bend of Sam's neck.

The phone rang and Mary answered. It was Grandmother asking what must she do, and Sam shot back, via Mary, for her, for goodness' sakes, not to *do* anything except stay put until the birds had gone away. Meanwhile the scene outside the window was mounting in its ferocity. The starving birds were in a frenzy to get at the meat and, barring that, at each other.

As the girls and I watched, Sam held and stroked and cajoled. Finally he persuaded John to turn his head and look. Tear-streaked and hiccuping with fright, our reluctant three-year-old turned his face toward the window. Still holding with death grip to his father's neck, he hung there, but he watched. It was a spectacle none of us had ever seen before.

It had been no more than ten minutes since I had heard John's first scream, but what had been our holiday turkey was now lying in the iris bed, picked as clean and blanched as white as if it had been left all year in the elements. All of the skin and scraps that Laura Lee had dropped in her retreat were gone, only a few grease spots on the walkway bearing witness to the fact that they had ever even been there in the first place.

Then, as quickly as they had apparently come, the birds left. The blackness lifted, turned, banked, and was gone. Behind them, scattered along the path and in Sam's bordering beds, they had left the bodies of eight or nine of their fellows, either already dead or dying. There was no other sign.

Across the way, we could see Granny watching through her windows. She waved, and Sam insisted until John hesitantly returned her greeting with a timid one of his own.

113

The girls were all abuzz with what had happened. They couldn't let it alone. Why did it happen? Were birds always that fierce? Were they carnivores? How could they bear to eat their own kind, eat other birds? Why did everyone think birds were so wonderful and innocent? Why hadn't anyone ever told them in school about this? And on and on.

Sam answered a fair number of questions before he took his frequently held position that the Walt Disney approach had done more harm to reality and probably to religion than anything since hard liquor, at which time the children backed off until Nora came home and the whole thing had to be told again.

During all the telling and the retelling and even through the paternal answers, John had been biding his peace, but I could tell that in his own three-year-old way he was listening and figuring. What he was figuring I couldn't tell, and I obviously wasn't to know.

The next day when lunchtime came and John had still not joined Sam junior and Vickie in going to Granny's, she called and extended him his own personal invitation to join her and Sam junior for a snack of pimiento cheese (his favorite) sandwiches and Kool-Aid. John told me to tell her no thank you, he didn't think so. I did and waited. The next day, the same thing. No trips outside and certainly no trips down the path to Granny's. On the third day, Saturday, I decided I had to attack the problem head on.

"All right, son," I said in my most authoritative voice. "We're going to your grandmother's."

"No, m'am, we're not," was his answer as he sat down on the floor and eyed me with something that lay somewhere between suspicion and open defiance.

"Yes, sir, we are." And go we did, but not before I had sworn to go every step of the way with him and not before I had agreed to let him wear his baseball cap with the broad bill.

And so it was to be all that winter and into the next spring. John wanted to go to Granny's just as much and just as frequently as ever, but he would not go unless someone took him and he would not go unless he had on his hat.

So far as I know, he never had nightmares about the birds.

He certainly refused to have any discussion about them or about our Thanksgiving afternoon; but he held on to his fear with a desperation that was as great as was his dependency on his protective cap and the comfort of an adult hand down the path.

By the following summer when he was busy turning four and being in his first real summer as a little boy and not a baby, he began to show less concern about the backyard. For one thing, the municipal authorities had done some active bird control for public health reasons, so there were just plain fewer birds to be afraid of. For another, juvenile memories are short and summer's days are long, like its pleasures. And, perhaps most significantly, I think he simply accepted his own fear sometime during that summer and decided to live with it as a nuisance but not an obstacle.

That kind of resolution comes more easily and at a younger age in a big family. Older and far superior (just ask them) siblings repeatedly shame the young into a courage and an acceptance that the single or small-family child often misses until later in life. Whatever happened and whatever sibling sadism may have contributed to his progress, by his fourth Thanksgiving John was crossing back and forth to Granny's as intrepidly as he ever had—maybe even more so, his father said, for now he knew that there were dangers everywhere and had chosen to go anyway.

Which kind of courage is, of course, the only usable kind, as John observed the other day when Mary reminded him that he had to register with the Selective Service on his birthday. "Yeah," he said, turning to look deeply and quietly at me. "Kinda makes you think of those Thanksgiving starlings, doesn't it, Maw?" Then he added, almost as if he were himself surprised. "They're sure a damned peculiar thing to be thankful for, but I guess I am."

And I know, truth told, as I look at my son, I'm thankful too—not just for him, but for all the pain and all the God-given starlings that have gone into making him strong and tall and just enough afraid so as always to be a man of courage.

13

Two Tickles
and Many Worlds

Sam junior and I are writing a book together, which in and of itself is a bit of a novelty for our family. Not the part about writing books—I do that most of my waking hours already; and as for Sam junior, he has been writing books since he was old enough to hold a crayon. It's the together part which is the novelty.

Sam junior's most serious effort at book writing, prior to our immediate joint endeavor, was called *The Book of Monsters* and was finished before he went to school. I have it now, put away in the front room chest along with the other serious memorabilia I have squirreled back over the years.

The Book of Monsters was and is considerably more than the usual child's book. Carefully bound—well, as carefully as any five-year-old hands can bind anything—and exhibiting an almost genetic command of bibliographic form on its title page, its copyright page, and its half-title page, *Monsters* goes on to become a catalog of some of the most believable spooks, ghouls, and dwarves ever to surface from dreamland. It was *Monsters*, in fact, that first let me guess that someday its author and I would write a book together; that's why it got saved in the front room chest. In a house of seven children, it's got to be good to get a spot on the refrigerator door for a couple of days. It has to be really ominous to earn eternity in the front room chest. *Monsters* qualified.

The book we are writing has to do with monsters itself, although somewhat secondarily. It really has to do with two worlds, our mortal one and the primordial one of creation. Every time someone observes that the only frontier we have left is inner space, I think maybe the book Sam junior and I are writing is really about three worlds, which it very well may be and which I may someday say . . . as soon as we are far enough into the writing for me to ascertain whether the inner world and the primordial world are or are not the same space. But that's another story.

Until I can solve the problem of inner space, then, Sam junior and I are presently working together on a book about two worlds. It is a book for kids his age (fifteen) and slightly younger, and it is as much fiction as anything ever really can be, which also is a debatable point as well as the one toward which all of this is going.

The more we work on building our imaginary world and describing its populace, the more my mind, and his father's, return to a day not more than two or three years ago when Sam junior was twelve or thirteen and had his first conscious, non-book experience with two worlds.

It was hot—blazingly, sullenly, miserably hot as only West Tennessee can be. Even the birds were tired, it was so hot. A television crew from Nashville was driving in that afternoon to do an on-site filming and interview about my work. The producer had already called ahead to say that they wanted to do mostly outdoor shots of the Lucy Goose, and I had, to no avail, run out all my reasons why that was not a great idea. They were coming two hundred miles, crew, van, and cameras, and they were going to do this thing their way, which meant outside.

Wondering if they really knew what dripping authors looked like on camera, especially when viewed by the cool and comfortable in their air-conditioned dens, I gave up and set about doing the charitable thing. I put Cokes in to chill, made fresh tea, checked the cookie supply, and wisely refrigerated extra beer.

117

Three of the children were home—John, Sam junior, and Becca. I hollered at them to turn the air-conditioning down because we were about to have some really hot souls, including their mother, on our hands; to change their clothes to the coolest things they owned because the producer, who had already indicated that she wanted shots of the children, was going to work outside instead of in; and in general to gird up their loins for a slight change of plans. We had to then go through the whole panoply from them of all the things I had already said to the producer, including the one about the dripping authors and their equally dripping kids not making good copy. Likewise to no avail.

So they got ready and we waited, and in time the mobile unit drove up the drive. The crew came in the house (I was grateful) for the introductions and the preliminaries, but all too soon it was out to work we go, four Tickles and three folks from video land, seven little dwarves in all.

By necessity of my profession, the children had been here before and knew what to expect. John easily set about helping with stringing electric cable and Sam junior to hauling and fetching from the van as instructed. We got set up with their help and ready to go. Becca, never one to be left out of anything, had apparently grown restive under her lack of responsibility and had gone back in for her egg basket. It was, by that time, well after three o'clock and close to the time that she would have had to go for it anyway, so I thought nothing about her actions.

I sat down, as instructed, in the patio glider with the fields behind me and my face to the camera while the talk show's hostess began a very well thought-out and concise set of questions about the writing. Into maybe the fourth or fifth question, I suddenly heard the producer say "Cut! Hold it right there!" Then turning to me, she said, "What's that child doing?"

I looked and all I could see was Sam junior standing on one side of the cameras and John still holding some cable. Turning to look behind me, however, I saw Becca opening the hen lot fence to come out, basket in hand. "Bringing in the eggs?" I offered.

"But that's great!" she said. "She cut right behind you a few minutes ago, but we can edit that out. I want a full shot of her going in there for real. Tell her to come back here and do it again."

"Becca," I called. "Put those eggs back in the nest and come here."

"Say what?"

"I said, put those eggs back where you got them and come here."

"You gotta be kidding," she hollered back, but she did it.

We stopped the interview and turned the cameras on Becca. She dutifully walked back again from the kitchen door to the hen lot, the cameras trained deliberately on her this time; but something went awry . . . the light, the voltage, the gods, who knows. Anyway, the take was no good and we had to call her back again. This time she made it all the way into the hen house and back out with the eggs before things went sour. And so it went for a good ten minutes.

Four times Becca replaced the eggs and re-gathered them before there was enough footage to make sure good editing could happen. John plainly thought it was funny. (The wisp of a smile with which he shows genuine amusement was playing all over his lower lip and chin.) Becca plainly did not. But Sam junior was a whole different study. I couldn't tell what he was thinking, but whatever it was, it was dark and disturbing.

Since the interview segment was already interrupted, the producer elected to go on with some other outdoor shots before we got back to literature. She wanted John doing something next. John was at that time at least fifteen, and on a farm there's very little a man can do that a fifteen-year-old boy isn't expected to do, none of it very easy to just suddenly up and do.

John did the logical thing. He walked to the shed and got the snathe with which we clear the fence lines and began to snathe. It is a job that the men do no more than twice in a summer and it is hardly serious labor. But John rightly surmised (and the producer followed his lead) that if shot cor-rectly, snathing could look more rural and more appropriate than it actually is. The trick worked, and twenty feet of fencerow near the hen house got a butch cut it hadn't expected and that the rest of the row didn't get—an aesthetic disfigurement that Sam made John amend after supper, but that's a different story too.

Then we got to Sam junior, who was looking all the while more distressed. "Can Becca take the eggs back into the hen lot while he waters the ducks and chickens and then helps her wash the eggs off?" our producer asked.

"You're kidding!" was his immediate response. "We don't wash the eggs out here. You'll break 'em if you do. And Becca won't wash 'em anyway. She's scared she'll get dirty. I have to do that!" He was truly aggrieved.

"Sam," I said with that quiet authority which is really scary, even to me, when I use it. "Do as she says."

"But, Mama!"

"Sam."

"Yes'm." And he did it . . . three times he did it before the two of them got it right. And twice he raked up the Johnson grass John had snathed and twice he scattered it back, but he plainly was not happy, a development that seemed to add even more humor to John's lower lip and chin. He more and more clearly thought this whole thing was a hoot.

Then it was my turn. Would I please go feed the chickens? Now if there is any of God's creatures that I truly despise, it's a chicken. I don't even like to eat them, for goodness' sakes, and the children know it. But I was certainly not involved in that contradiction at the moment. I simply went into the hen house, brought up a gallon tin of feed from the barrels, and began to scatter the scratch while the cameras ground.

"That's it! That does it!" Sam junior said as he turned, stormy-faced and scowling, toward the kitchen door. In he went, and we saw no more of Sam junior.

Eventually we went back to the interview, which even after the interruption was fun to do. The crew had done their homework and knew what they were asking about and how to ask in order to get what they wanted. A good interviewer, as any writer will tell you, is as rare as a good editor and just as valuable. This one was good. So the afternoon went quickly and time slid by so smoothly that I never even got around to the beer and Cokes before our guests had to load up and go. John helped them repack, and Becca carried her weary eggs to the refrigerator. Still no Sam junior.

The minute the van was gone, however, and we were back in the house, my son was there, facing me down in my own kitchen.

"How could you!" he said.

"How could I what?"

"How could you stand there and let them do that to us?"

"What in the world," I asked in irritation, "did I *let* them do?"

"That was all a bunch of lies—just lies!" His lip was trembling just ever so slightly, and I realized for the first time that his face was blanched white and his cheekbones dyed fiery red. This was not temper, however, although he is perfectly capable of that. No, the tear caught in the inside corner of his left eye said that this was rage or pain or both. John had apparently arrived at the same conclusion. I heard him cut behind us and slip down the stairs to his room where he quickly shut the door.

"That was no lie, son."

"That *was* lies! Every bit of it. You made Becca gather those damned eggs four times! That's a lie. John never snathes that back fence. We use the hand mower on that part and you know it. We don't wash eggs out there either and"—this was apparently the worst offense of all—"and you *hate* chickens!" He was defiant.

Now this was a child, as I have said, who grew up on television production. Had he never seen a camera before or a TV crew or a mobile unit, I could have understood. But he knew what all those things are. That's what led me to make a tactical mistake.

"But you know as well as I do that the intent of what they were doing is the truth—the effect is accurate. That's what matters—that the end result must be credible as well as accurate. You know as well as I do that they kill and re-kill

121

every single drug dealer on 'Miami Vice' about a dozen times before they let the poor boob call it a day and go home, and you don't ever say that that's a lie." (Parental logic is a good and blessed thing, just not worth a damn.)

"But that's not us. That's a show and this is our family!"

Good point. Even I had to admit that it was a good point. For the next hour and until well after Sam got home, I had to admit it was a good point . . . not a valid one, but an emotionally logical one.

As with a lot of the real stuff of living, we never resolved his problem. After a while, I ran out of words with which to try, he ran out of energy with which to hurt, and Sam senior ran out of patience with which to await our dinner. We ate and cleaned up and carefully walked around the problem for a few days until time had done its magic of making the conflict less intense.

So now we are writing a book together, he and I, and it's a fantasy about at least two worlds. Before we get much farther into the work, he's going to have to start doing some of the scripting of the events in the story himself. When that happens, he's going to discover that all the events and all the people he can imagine, invent, or describe are people and events he has in some way known.

He's going to have to make his peace with the fact that writing—that creating in any medium—is simply the art of adjusting for the greatest clarity the givens you've already received . . . which is why every fantasy book, or any piece of any art for that matter, is really about God. It is also why artists are better hawkers for the Kingdom than preachers are. The priest may be the main attraction inside the tent, but nine times out of ten it's art that drew the crowd in.

There is an interesting corollary to this, of course, in that the pseudo-preacher has to use pseudo-art to sucker his following. Sam junior certainly knows enough about television to have figured that out for himself by now. Maybe I will start there with him . . . or maybe I will just jump

122

right in and ask him outright to tell me how many of those original fishers of men were ordained preachers. Whatever else I do, I certainly plan to ask him why, in his opinion, the Son of God was incarnated as a craftsman. Then we'll just have to see how the rest of it goes on from there.

Of Tailless Kites
and Naked Ladies

R ebecca was ten during what I now refer to as the Year of the Kites. As the long, gray days of a preternaturally delayed spring stretched farther and farther that year into late April, so the kite season was preternaturally stretched at our house. The turbulence of the air rushing from the sunning earth up to the still chilly sky had already carried two kites—one homemade and loved, the other bought and much envied—to an appropriate end high in the pin oaks below the pond.

And day after day, as I watched from the kitchen window in the late afternoons, Rebecca followed her string across the field while high above her head yet another kite now bobbed frantically, struggling for the absolute freedom of broken string. As the kite bobbed, its tail would cavort behind it, keeping it earthbound so that it could the more effectively strain toward heaven.

This particular tail had to be, by any set of criteria, the ugliest tail a kite has ever had, an observation that even Rebecca kept making every afternoon as she headed outdoors, kite and tail in hand, toward the open field. I don't know as it was a complaint so much as it was a neutral observation on her part. The kite had an ugly tail. It had been made of pieces of an old T-shirt tied into a trail of old sheet, both being gray and porous from wear and washing. And both, against the flamboyant blue and plastic red of the kite's dragon, were too tired to even be tawdry. All the tail meant to Rebecca was that Daddy, three kites later, had grown weary of kites for that year, at least too weary to bring any real imagination to bear on another tail.

The first day she had had this one she had tried, in her disappointment, to take the tail off. Despite my assurances that it would run out of control and flightless without the gray poverty behind it, she had to see for herself. Twenty minutes later she came sorrowfully back in the kitchen door, went to her room and quietly tied the tail back in place. Thus her daily observation that it was the ugliest tail a kite ever had was always laced more with resignation than with any critical complaint.

My own feeling about the kite with the infamous tail was a bit more focused in a diffuse sort of way. The transit of the tail from house to field and field back to house concurred almost exactly each afternoon with the evening news telecast.

The little black-and-white set on the kitchen counter diverts my attention from the tedium of cooking supper, but the details of cooking supper seem also to blur some of my grasp of the news. Thus a portion of my perception of the kite's tail was mixed that year by its temporal proximity with carrot peels and the latest coverage of the crackdown on *Penthouse* and *Playboy*. The issues of First Amendment rights versus Bible Belt rectitude bounced back and forth across the screen as first one side was interviewed and then the other. From across the carrot peels both sides looked slightly polyester and remarkably alike.

It was always at just such moments that Rebecca would come back in each afternoon to get ready for supper. She would walk through the kitchen, kite in tow, shaking her head and muttering, "Ugliest tail I ever saw, but it sure takes a little tail to make the sucker fly." As I flushed the peels down the disposal, I frequently would observe to myself that Rebecca was probably wiser than at least one half of the folk being interviewed on the evening news.

It is for that reason, of course, that I have stopped cooking supper. We're having carrots again tonight for the first time in

125

quite a while, and peeling them just now made me remember. So I have turned off the stove and sat down to write while memory is still fresh in my mind.

Rebecca was thirteen last spring. She too, the seventh and the last of them, is growing up. Someday soon she is going to meet evil—adult evil—and she is going to have to understand for herself its functions and origins. She is going to have to discover all over again, as we all must, the lines that divide morality from religion. I cannot help her in that chore, cannot go with her, cannot do it for her. But I can turn off my stove and sit down to write for her a story about some April afternoons when, as a child, she once had understood.

—— 15 ——

Anybody Seen a Lutheran Lately?

*A*lex Haley's Henning, Tennessee, where Chicken George's descendants and Haley's cousins still live, is only a short hike up Highway 51 North from Lucy, Tennessee, where the Lucy Goosey Farm is and I live. Once, when we were at a meeting together somewhere and were swapping stories in the way of Southerners who are eternally homesick, he said to me: "Lucy? I remember Lucy. It was just like Henning. Everybody was a Baptist, a Church of Christ, or a cow, and you knew them all the same."

We got a good laugh as one is supposed to do when one is tale-swapping with a compatriot. I assured him that things have not changed substantially in Lucy just as they have not in Henning, except, as we both remarked, that there's been a growth, over the years, in Methodists and pickup trucks in both places.

If we were to have the same conversation now, I would also have to tell him that there have been further changes, at least in Lucy—this time, a decline in cows and a measurable rise in Episcopalians. Whether the two events are related or not, of course I can't say, but they are contemporaneous. In fact, our situation has been shifting in that direction for a year or two now—Baptists, Church of Christ, Methodists, cows, pickups, and Episcopalians in pretty much that order. It leaves out a lot—goats, station wagons, and Lutherans, for instance.

I can't say that I have ever been more than casually concerned, however, with either the percentages or the omissions until fairly recently. The taller of our two Roman Catholic sons-in-law has for years contended that the Episcopal Church is simply the Republican Party at prayer, no more and no less—an observation with which he is pleased to bait me whenever there is a lag in the conversation or a new book of mine has just come out. So I should have had reason to at least passingly consider the increasing suburbanization and Episcopalizing of our village; but, as always, I had been far too busy reading about the world to give any thought to looking at my own small part of it until two weeks ago.

It was a cold, horrendously windy night, and a new book had indeed just been published the week before. To celebrate and to raise some money for autistic children in our area, the women of our parish had planned a literary evening. I was to read from the new book and then afterwards we would sell books at the customary wine and cheese reception.

We were all encouraged by the advance ticket sales, and the biting weather was in our favor—too cold to do anything outdoors but too near spring to love an open fire and a quiet night at home. So, by seven-thirty the nave of the church was pretty well filled to capacity, and I began the usual chatter with which any speaker tries to warm his audience and win their affection.

In the course of my opening, I made my completely thought-free comments about no Lutherans in Lucy, quipping to a grinning audience that if there were indeed one of Martin's followers among us, I wished he or she would hold up his hand for he probably was the only one in north Shelby County. Getting the required laugh and the expected dearth of hands, I pushed on to the real business of the evening and began the reading.

Afterward we all adjourned to the year's most elegant party, at least for our township, with enough good wine and exquisite cheeses to content any gourmet. Even the men had pitched in with flower arrangements and some needed refurbishing of the parish hall, so that the whole effect was one of community and jollity with no thought of Lutherans . . . until the next Sunday.

It was the first Sunday of Lent and I was the lector for the eleven o'clock service. In the Women's Robing Room (as the sign on the door chooses to denominate what is at best no more than an overgrown closet) we were engaged in the intimacy of seven women struggling in an eight-by-six-foot space to find vestments that were both the right fit and the right color at the same time.

Robing is one of the least attractive moments of any Sunday for me. I frequently think that any honest atheist would have a heyday of pleasure if he could only see our semi-nude frustration as we elbow our way around one another toward the ecclesiastical proprieties. Certainly even the godly would chuckle if they could see the soloist with the cassock's closures hooked in her bouffant or the lector hung by a bra strap caught on a shoulder tie.

Finally we were all done and the choir pushed on out ahead of me. Snapping the last hole in my ridiculously medieval attire, I turned to follow them when I realized that Maria was still just outside the doorway. Red-robed for the choir, she was almost breathtakingly beautiful. A relative newcomer, she and her husband had just begun their family—a baby girl born in late December—and her body still had that soft, rounded slowness that pregnancy and first childbirth give to deeply feminine women. They had both been in school in Michigan and had only come here to his home and new jobs at the first of the year. Already, though, they had joined his parents in being actively involved in parish life. She was not only in the choir, but also taking instruction to be confirmed in the Episcopal Church. I liked her instinctively and unreservedly, but I was surprised to see her still there and obviously waiting.

"I enjoyed Friday night," she said.

"Yes, it was fun, wasn't it?" I knew that this wasn't what we were really here to talk about. She hesitated.

"When you said that about Lutherans . . . ?"

My word, I thought to myself in that moment of horror that accompanies the amnesia of any public performance, what have I gone and said about Lutherans? One of Sam's older brothers lived and died a converted Lutheran and obviously, therefore, one of my favorite sisters-in-law is a devout Lutheran. What awful thing have I unwittingly said about Lutherans?

She must have read my distress, because she shook her head. "No. Just when you said that if there were any Lutherans in the place, you wished they'd hold up their hands because they'd be the only ones in Lucy."

"Yes," I said, and then I saw the tears swimming up, threatening to spill and irreparably spot the robe beneath. "It's OK," she said, swiping at them and smiling just a little. "It's just that I am one, and I wish I could talk to one before I change."

Oh, Father, I thought, how many places can we hurt in and invent to hurt each other in. New baby, new house, new job, new state, new family, new church. Of course she wanted to see another Lutheran before she changed! I wanted to hug her, but she had already stepped back as if wary that I might.

"Why don't you?" I said instead.

"Because, like you said, there aren't any." She grinned more openly. The last of the choir was moving out of the hall and heading for the narthex. "It may all be the same God," she said quickly as she started toward their retreating line, "but it really is the how-you-get-at-Him that makes it home."

At best calculation Maria is thirty-odd years my junior, but I never heard anyone cut the form of religion more cleanly from its center, like the Easter ham from its bone, than she did in that brief moment. Still arrested by her, I made my way thoughtfully down the short hall to join the back of the processional, the hem of my black robe flapping jovially around my ankles and teasing the arches of my feet. She had been right, of course. I fuss about the vestments and the liturgical proprieties, but they are home for me. She was also right that the pain for any of us of whatever age is learning to take God as home instead of the familiar as god.

16

Credo Ergo Sum

J ohn is tearing down the old turkey lot this summer in his spare time and along with the rest of his chores. It is kind of his gift to me. To be perfectly honest, I think the rest of this family could look at the thing in perpetuum without a qualm, but it bothers me.

The thing sits at the upper end of the back pasture and right at the outside side of the backyard fence, where—or this was the theory in the beginning—it would be as handy as the chicken house, which sits in almost the same position on the west side of the yard but securely inside the backyard fence. Turkeys, like chickens, are too dumb to be believed. As a result, both have to be kept near enough so one does not lose one's whole enthusiasm for Thanksgiving and Christmas just because raising the traditional feast is such a bloody nuisance.

Our turkeys, in particular, were always needful of human help. I can remember one whole hatching one year that never learned to roost. The result was that somebody—usually Sam junior, bless him—had to go out every night and pick up all those half-grown and evil-dispositioned critters and set them up on some perch or other inside the lot so they could sleep. This he or his relief crew did every night for months until the holidays finally came and took care of the problem by granting the birds eternal repose.

It was during that summer of child-dependent roosting, in fact, that Sam senior finally gave up all hope of keeping the turkey-keepers from climbing over his back fence. He decided, instead, to open up a gate so that they could pass more easily back and forth to their charges. This he did, in what seemed a most logical manner to us, by taking out a section of the rail fencing and replacing it with an Appalachian gate, although at the time we didn't know that that was what our walk-through was.

In the mountains where we grew up and Sam learned his style of farming, folks make what they call a walk-through and what is now called, in the village of Lucy at least, an Appalachian gate. Once a section of fence has been removed, a new fence post is planted halfway across the opened space. Two more posts are planted about two and a half to three feet to the north and to the south of the new post respectively, and in a straight line out from above or below it, as the case may be. One side of the original fence is then continued a half-a-length to the new middle post, leaving a half-a-section opening with a post on each side of it. A new and full section of fence is then built from the last post of the other part of the original fence out to both the new north and new south posts.

The result of all this effort is a kind of bisected "y" or "v", depending on whether or not one considers the tail of existing fence as a part of the configuration. The result is also a walk-through, as even a flatlander can plainly see if he looks at one. Most animals, especially the kind one keeps in with fences, can't turn sharp corners and people can. Thus the name and the function.

The odd thing about Sam's walk-through was that we didn't know it was unusual until our near neighbor came to have a look and then our next beyond him and then another, until it finally dawned on us we should dignify the thing with some sort of name. Since we couldn't patent it, we christened it instead, giving it its current appellation of "Appalachian gate." There are more than a few now scattered throughout the village, and Sam looks at every one of them with a paternal pride. Thus, whatever John does about the turkey lot, he has been told very specifically that he cannot tear down the first, and prototypal, Appalachian gate in Lucy.

Actually what John does is already close to being what John has done. He took the pickup around through the orchard gate and up into the upper pasture the other day after work, tied a rope to the hitch and another to the back corner post and drove off again. The post, half rotten at best, snapped off, but it had the grace to snap at ground level and to bring several others with it as it came. It will be a matter now of only about two Saturdays' work to get all the posts and wire meshing and doors and planks pulled loose and scooped up for a trip or two to the county dump, and then I shall be rid of the lot, if not of turkeys, for the rest of this life anyway.

We haven't raised turkeys in quite a while. Not only are they very stupid and consequently very time-consuming to raise, but they are also one of those things we have outgrown the need of . . . that is to say, raising them is. When we came to the farm, no small part of our motivation was, as I have said, the business of teaching our children how to do it, that and the business of teaching them that everything is bought at a price—if not with Daddy's money, then with the labor it represents. Nothing so decreases one's consumerist passions as a cocktail of sweat every night before supper.

But the point has been made, and continuing to raise what can more cheaply be bought already full-grown is itself silly. So now we eat our turkeys from the supermarket and raise only thistle and stinkweed in the turkey lot.

Neither thistle nor stinkweed has ever needed a lot of protection in order to thrive, but it has been truly amazing to me to see what proportions both can arrive at when protected as they have been within the confines of the old turkey lot . . . which was why I wanted it down. Every time I looked out my kitchen window, or wanted to show a friend the Appalachian gate, or even tried to enjoy a doze in the hammock, all I saw or smelled was that crop of thistles and stinkweed growing higher and higher in the turkey run. So, although John has not totally taken down the turkey lot yet, he has, in the sense of cleaning up the mess, already pulled the thing down below sight level and thereby earned my gratitude.

133

The turkey lot is the first of our additions to the Lucy Goosey to go, to be thrown out, to be folded away. It is not an unpleasant feeling, in fact, to know that something we built and needed and used is no longer needed; that we have grown out of a phase or stage of life in which it was needed.

I've been doing a lot of that kind of folding away in the last couple of years indoors, of course: giving Nora the *Britannica Junior* and the old *Every Child's Illustrated* for her family, for instance, because nobody here can function at that level anymore; passing the last of the bicycles out to flea markets because they have grown too small or too inconvenient compared to the new freedom of cars and driver's licenses. The lower shelves in the closets have one by one come out to make room for taller storage, and the last of the bathroom step stools turned up in the storage shed the other day when I was out there and stumbled on it in the dark.

So while the turkey yard is the first of the big things, the outdoor things, to go, it is certainly not the first in general; and it is indeed a good feeling. A perception of narrowing or of focus, of having completed something and of moving on to more focus. I was trying to tell John, when I was thanking him for the lot, about why it meant so much to me to have it gone.

"You just need so much less as you grow older," I said.

"Sounds awful," he said, his mind already on the L. L. Bean catalog that had come in the mail and was waiting for him on the kitchen table.

"I don't ever want to not want stuff," chimed in Rebecca.

"Sure you do," I said. "It's when you can get rid of the noise and the clutter and get it down to the essentials."

"And what's the essentials?" shot back Miss Thirteen and Wise.

"Just . . . just being," I said, and realized somewhat to my surprise that that has been true for some time now without my knowing it. I am, and it doesn't require all the creeds and hymns and theories that it used to take. The years and their love have replaced them. Now, standing in my own kitchen, looking at my Appalachian gate without its turkey lot, I believe, and *satis est*. It is enough.

17

The Sign of the Eagle

John is going off to college this year. At our house, as at most others, that effectively means that John is going.

He will come back, of course, in the sense that his leaving is not a severance of his roots from our soil; but he will have to think more and more each year from now on about when and how to come back. He will increasingly have to plan for the dates and means of coming back. He will have to work at us, in other words.

It is a shift in things that I have always found to be a little sad as well as a little hard because, although John doesn't know it yet, Sam and I will have to work at him more and more now. His coming will be something we have to check the dates on and arrange things for. And the conversations of his coming back will be, as they have been with Nora and Mary and Philip and Laura, active exercises in trying to reconnect when most of the pieces are missing. When experiences diverge, only the suprastructure of remembrance can cause them to converge again.

So I have spent these last few months telling John good-bye in ways he hasn't even caught me at, in all the subtle ways a mother has, in all the "Do you remembers?" that will be my touchstone in ten years when he comes back and doesn't know how to begin again.

135

Despite his innocence of what lies ahead and of the bridges I am so carefully building, John has been building a few of his own for future use, ones he doesn't yet understand the reasons for even as he is building them. Instinct, be it physical or spiritual, is a most wonderful thing and the freedom to follow it without self-editing, a most wonderful gift. John has it.

John is a country boy. He would hate to hear me say that because he is also very definitely a sophisticated kid who is as comfortable in the middle of Washington or Cincinnati as he is in the middle of a pasture. But the truth remains that he can gut and butcher a deer without direction; that he can run a tractor as well as his father can; that he can drop a squirrel at two hundred yards or heave a bale of hay for five—not one of which abilities is a function of urban life, whether John likes it or not.

Even more revealing is the fact that John tolerates only two pieces of jewelry. One is his watch. It cost him almost all of his first week's pay the summer he was fifteen and went to work during the day as a gofer for a construction crew.

The watch was one he had envied on his best friend and had longed for for two whole semesters. It not only tells the usual tales of time, date, seconds, and appointments; it also has a calculator that has tended to be invaluable in algebra, and a memory that stores more facts than I would have thought an IBM could house.

You ask John now for his Social Security number and he asks his watch; his checking account number and he punches his watch; our dental insurance policy number and he raises his wrist to inquire. Things have got to such a pitch, in fact, that I am hysterical if he leaves his watch at home when we go someplace together; and it is Mama who always goes instantly to town to buy new batteries when the thing on John's wrist begins to beep that the energy in its innards is getting low.

But John's other piece of finery is almost exactly the opposite of his watch. Around his neck, on a short, heavy chain and almost always deliberately hidden under his shirt, John wears his baptismal medal. I don't know, because I didn't buy it, but I suspect that the chain is made of some kind of steel or heavy alloy. Whatever its composition, it is certainly impervious to the obvious threats of John's life-style. He bought the chain, just as he also paid to have the medal soldered to it, with some of his money from this summer's job as a carpenter's assistant, and he has worn it consistently ever since. The medal is intimately tied to John's leaving.

We are not, as you know, Roman Catholic at our house, but Episcopalian (or, as our bishops are fond of saying, Anglo-Catholic. It is a small point to most folks and not one I have ever been too eager to belabor publicly, although at home we have always tried to make the distinction clear to the children). As Episcopalians—or Anglo-Catholics, if you prefer—we baptize our children under their given names and not under a saint's. When, therefore, John was baptized, he was baptized as John because it was his name and his grandfather's name before him. Because it was also a liturgical name, however, he, more or less by default, assumed all the icons and churchly heritage of St. John, the Gospeler, the apostle, the author of the Apocalypse, the beloved of Our Lord.

Such a thing is a heavy accretion to lay upon an eight-pound baby, if one thinks about it much. To be honest, I didn't. I simply accepted in his name and stored for safekeeping and his future use the gifts that he received on his christening day, including his baptismal medal.

Flat, square, and small—no more than three-quarters of an inch in any given direction—and fashioned in sterling silver, it shows the head, beak, and upper wing curvature of a ferocious, handsome, and watchful eagle. Across the lower portion of the eagle's feathered chest is a scroll that reads simply "St. John" and bears the sign of the cross beside the name. On the back, the givers, dear friends of many years standing, had had "J.C.T. 7/11/70" engraved in an Old English script. Only this and nothing more, to quote Poe.

Afraid that as an infant he would swallow the medal or hurt himself trying, I had put it away with the rest of his keepsakes. From time to time over the years of his infancy and boyhood,

I would show it to him and tell him who St. John was. As he grew older, he would sometimes ask to have something by or about St. John as his choice for our evening story time, but he never asked about the eagle.

Like most Episcopalian kids, long after the Thanksgiving of the starlings and long before his present level of maturity, John got churched—or at least the church made a pass at trying to get his attention.

He went through weeks of instruction, which finally culminated in his confirmation and his admission to holy communion. How much of it took and how much has yet to take is anybody's guess and probably none of anybody's business, at least not at the moment. But he did, in the process, get introduced to symbols, including the centuries-old symbols or icons of the Evangelists—the man, the lion, the winged ox, and the eagle. That took. It took right in my kitchen, right in the middle of my canning the first of that particular spring's peaches.

"Why do you suppose folks took animals as signs for Saints Matthew, Mark, Luke, and John?" was how he began.

"I don't know. What does Father King say about it?"

"Says because symbols were safer than words when the Christians were being persecuted."

"Don't you believe that?"

"Yeah, why not? But why animals? Why not things?"

"Did you ask?"

"Yeah."

"Well?" This was getting to be an exasperating conversation, and I didn't envy any priest who had to take a bunch of twelve-year-olds through the process two or three times every year of his clerical life.

"Well, he said he thought I ought to be asking why the Indians didn't use things instead of animals for their totem poles."

"Holy Toledo!" I said, not having expected so direct an answer and having burned myself on hot peach syrup as a result.

"Yeah, that's what I said," my son responded, and went off to ponder something more accessible and less dangerous.

Sometime later—I don't remember when, I just recall that it was cold outside and wintry enough so that John was in instead of out that afternoon—I asked him about the Indians.

"Appears to me," he said thoughtfully, "as if a person would probably be a lot more comfortable being a bear than a bow and arrow, 'specially since a bear can move on its own hook without having to have another Indian around."

"I'll buy that," I said.

"Except, of course," he continued without even noticing me, "that the real question is, What's so good about being a bear—other than the fact that it beats being a bow and arrow?"

"Well, I can certainly understand that," I said. End of conversation and end of my active memory of the whole until this summer when John came and asked me for his baptismal medal.

"Sure," I said, getting it out of my jewelry box and giving it to him. "But what do you want it for?"

"Oh," he said with an elaborate casualness. "I guess I just feel more like being an eagle now than I used to." The piece of fashioned silver slipped deftly into his jeans pocket. "Thanks for keeping it for me all these years," he added as he turned and left the room.

Which was last June and the end of that conversation until one day last week when John leaned over to lift a box for me and the medal fell out, as it does from time to time, from under his shirt. As he set the box in place on the shop table, he stood back, dusted his hands and unconsciously raised his right hand to drop the medal back under his T-shirt. I caught his hand as it went toward the medal.

"Want to tell me why now?" I asked.

He grinned, the dimple he used to hate and his girlfriend now adores deepened to frame his lower face. He shrugged. "I guess it's kind of like your wedding ring," he said. "Kind of a calling, the cross and the eagle and my name on there all together . . . kind of a calling."

139

Well, son, may it be a good calling, as good and as full as your father's and mine have been. May it bring you home from time to time and, more important, may it carry you far away again. May it teach you praise and cause you to worship, and may it, in the end, also be a holy vocation.